ROUTLEDGE LIBRARY EDITIONS:
TRADE UNIONS

I0127635

Volume 15

MODERN TRADE
UNIONISM

MODERN TRADE UNIONISM

A Study of the Present Tendencies and the future of Trade Unions in Britain

J. T. MURPHY

Routledge
Taylor & Francis Group

LONDON AND NEW YORK

First published in 1935 by George Routledge & Sons Ltd.

This edition first published in 2023
by Routledge
4 Park Square, Milton Park, Abingdon, Oxon OX14 4RN

and by Routledge
605 Third Avenue, New York, NY 10158

Routledge is an imprint of the Taylor & Francis Group, an informa business

© 1935 J. T. Murphy

British Library Cataloguing in Publication Data
A catalogue record for this book is available from the British Library

ISBN: 978-1-032-37553-3 (Set)
ISBN: 978-1-032-39428-2 (Volume 15) (hbk)
ISBN: 978-1-032-39438-1 (Volume 15) (pbk)
ISBN: 978-1-003-34971-6 (Volume 15) (ebk)

DOI: 10.4324/9781003349716

Publisher's Note
The publisher has gone to great lengths to ensure the quality of this reprint but points out that some imperfections in the original copies may be apparent.

Disclaimer
The publisher has made every effort to trace copyright holders and would welcome correspondence from those they have been unable to trace.

MODERN TRADE
UNIONISM

A Study of the present tendencies
and the future of Trade Unions
in Britain

By

J. T. MURPHY

LONDON

GEORGE ROUTLEDGE AND SONS, LTD.

BROADWAY HOUSE: 68–74 CARTER LANE, E.C.

1935

PRINTED IN GREAT BRITAIN BY
STEPHEN AUSTIN AND SONS, LIMITED, HERTFORD.

CONTENTS

AUTHOR'S PREFACE

A BOOK which purports to discuss some of the most important problems of Modern Trade Unionism cannot help raising many new questions concerning other institutions, especially when the answers given to the Trade Union problems visualize the coming of a new society in which the economic and social foundations, and therefore the structure, will be different from those of to-day. To attempt to answer all the new questions concerning the effect of, for example, " Workers' Control of Industry " on the Parliamentary Institution and various State departments would be interesting and worth while.

But although I am conscious that these questions do arise, I have in this book necessarily confined myself to dealing with the Trade Unions, their structure, policy, and future in relation to the coming of Socialism, and in no sense have I attempted to give a complete picture of the structure of Socialist society.

In its critical aspects, the book is intended as

a challenge to those who, I think, under-estimate the future of the Trade Unions. In its positive aspects it is a call to the workers in industry to make the Trade Unions into more effective instruments of the struggle for Socialism.

I wish to thank Mr. H. N. Brailsford for his helpful foreword, and Mr. William Mellor, Mr J. F. Horrabin, and Mr. F. W. Hickinbottom for their useful criticisms and suggestions.

J. T. M.

FOREWORD

By H. N. BRAILSFORD

THE Socialist Movement has suffered from the fact that most of its thinking and writing has been done for it by men and women who belong to " professional " groups. We contend, and with truth, that we are workers : no miner or ploughboy has ever worked harder or more productively than Karl Marx or Sidney and Beatrice Webb. No reasonable being questions our sincerity ; for few of us have anything tangible to gain from the changes we advocate. But we lack most of the experiences that make the outlook of the manual worker. Few of us have lived for long on the borderline of subsistence : none of us have been denied access to the intellectual heritage of mankind : none of us have felt the insult of an inferior status in society : something of all this we can conceive if we possess imagination. But how many of us ever grasp the significance of the chief formative experience through which in this country every worker in a well-organized trade must pass ? We can know the life of a Trade Union only from the outside. Some of us belong, as I do, to a professional Trade Union : a few conscious of the nature of their calling have become honorary gas workers. These substitutes can give us nothing of the reality. We do not know from our own daily lives what it means to a young worker to enter this disciplined army. We have never had to tighten our belts through a prolonged and doubtful strike. If we ever succeed in understanding the instinctive loyalty bred in a great union with a long tradition, we achieve it only as rare men sometimes manage to understand a woman's life. Without this experience it is difficult for the " intellectual " to grasp the meaning of the word " class ". He readily assents to the ideal of a class-less society. But does he ever realize the dynamic possibilities of " class " in the unequal society of to-day ? To feel " class ", to know it as a force in history, one must have stood in a queue at a paydesk, or better still in a strike picket, over against an employer with the police and the courts ranged behind him.

The lack of this experience makes us from the start " outsiders " in the Labour Movement.

We have, none the less, much to contribute.
We are usually more articulate with voice and
pen than the manual workers ; we are more
at home in the world of theory, and some of
us are by training organizers. We fling ourselves with ardour into the political life of the
Party, for in this field we know how to use our
tools. The result has been, I suspect, in this
country and in others, a steady over-emphasis
on the political aspects of the Socialist Movement. We who write, with few exceptions,
its books, pamphlets, and newspapers, have no
knowledge at first hand of the basic organization
of the working-class. The reader may reply
that our deficiencies are amply compensated by
the numerous Trade Union leaders who sit on all
the Party's benches in Parliament, including the
front bench. I am not sure that this is so.
Among these Trade Union leaders there are
and have been many able men of strong
character. Theirs, however, is usually a practical
ability. They are organizers and negotiators.
It is a rare chance if they combine with these
gifts an interest in theory, or the sceptical
habit of mind that questions current assumptions
and accepted tendencies.

The result is that the whole process of

reaching Socialism is conceived among us in political terms. A capitalist government, administering the present industrial system, must be peaceably replaced, or as the minority would say, violently overthrown, by a political party that will supply an alternative government. From this formula, it may be that there is no escape. But in our more detailed strategy have we ever perceived the part that Trade Unions should play ? The Russians when they made their social revolution based it and the whole permanent structure of their power on an improvised strike committee—for in origin that is what the Soviets were. In 1905, and again in 1917, when quasi-political strikes first shook and then overthrew Tsardom, the militant organization of the active mass of the workers in St. Petersburg and Moscow was an almost spontaneous gathering of delegates from the factories and later from the disaffected regiments. It came together naturally, without theory, an inevitable conclusion from the logic of events. Because it led and acted, and won the trust of the masses, it gathered round itself the legend, the aureole of victory that the Duma lacked. To it the instinctive loyalty of the workers responded.

There is a lesson here which we in this country have not sufficiently considered. It is gross stupidity to argue that what succeeded, in wholly different conditions, in Russia will succeed here. History and a widely different economic structure mock such reasoning. But in this instance the argument from history tells the other way. Ours is by far the older and more glorious Trade Union organization. It had been gathering to itself the hereditary loyalty of the workers for a century before the Labour Party existed. From its ranks the martyrs came. Round it gathered all the memories of an heroic struggle. If you would know which social unit, Party or Union, arouses in the worker's mind the stronger emotion of loyalty and militancy, carry your question to a mining village in Durham or Northumberland, where sons follow their father's trade. The Party makes an appeal to the head, but the Union with its stained and venerable banners touches every nerve in a worker's body, as the thought of the clan once did in the feudal Highlands. The appeal is weaker, no doubt, in trades less stoutly organized than mining is or was and the mobility of labour in the overgrown town can sap it. But it is, none the less, an emotional force that we have neglected. The art of politics is, I take it, mainly a skill in mobilizing, round the appropriate social units, the strongest human emotions.

These are vague and general considerations : what do they mean in the concrete ? They may conduct us, first of all, to some survey of the Trade Union structure itself. Is the organization that has grown up historically, whether we look at branch, trade, or industry, the best, not merely for the daily struggle, but for the ultimate effort, the conquest of power ? Can we get on a " shop " basis an organization incomparably more flexible, more militant, more adaptable to a political purpose than is usual to-day ? Again, are the Unions, all of them or most of them, doing all that they are best fitted to do for the political education and organization of their members ? What part might they have to play—by recruiting special constables for example—if ever a Socialist Government has to defend democratic order against a fascist threat ? Is there a place for the general strike in a Socialist strategy, and if so, under what conditions ? What changes in union structure may be necessary as we enter the phase of regulated industry, and where does the line of division fall between the militant organization that the industrial struggle demands, and the more specious forms of the corporative state ? What transformation of spirit, function, and structure will a Trade Union undergo, when within a socialized industry the class-less society is realized ? Finally, do we mean to build our system of representative government in the future socialist state on a functional or a territorial basis ? These are not questions of theory. They will answer themselves in one sense or the other, according to the part that Trade Unions actually play in our struggle for power.

An " outsider " can ask these questions. To answer them demands not merely a grasp of theory and history, but direct experience of union life in a manual trade. This it is that makes the value of J. T. Murphy's book. He is as familiar as any of us with the history and the theory. But, in addition, he possesses the living experience that the " professional " worker lacks. He played a distinguished part, as leader and pioneer, in the most interesting development of our time within Trade Unionism —the shop steward movement of the stormy war years. He has also the advantage of familiarity

with Russian experience. I met him first, as
it happens, in Moscow towards the end of the
civil war, in 1920. He has answered in the
following chapters the questions that I have
just raised, and on the whole, I think, convinc-
ingly. A set of dogmatic answers would be
useless. The merit of this study is that it
reasons candidly from intimate experience.

CHAPTER I

INTRODUCTION

THIS is not a history of Trade Unions. Were
it intended to be such it would of necessity
have to follow the course taken by Mr. and Mrs.
Sidney and Beatrice Webb in their historic
work *The History of Trade Unionism.* My plan
is much less ambitious. It is to examine in
an introductory way certain outstanding features
of the history of Trade Unions in order to
focus attention on their future.

This question is a debatable one. There
are those who think that the unions have no
future and regard them as declining institutions
which Fascism will finally abolish. There are
others who believe that there will be a growing
integration of the unions and the State and
a division of function between the State, the
employers' organizations, and the Trade Unions.
There are yet others who contemplate an
economic and social change so profound that
it will radically change the structure, character,
and purpose of the unions which will become

I   B

industrial bodies controlling the productive
processes within a socialist system.

It is the author's conviction that mankind is
travelling towards Socialism and, however it may
come, the Trade Unions must be transformed
to fulfil new functions. What these functions will be we shall discuss at length
especially in view of the conflicting theories
as to the meaning of " Workers' Control of
Industry ".

There are few to-day who will deny that
modern capitalist industry with its automatic
machine processes has a deadening effect upon
the great mass of the workers and that the
new body of technicians are a doubtful quantity
in their political affiliations because of the
uncertainty of their future. Can man become
the master of the machine and organize the
productive and distributive processes so that
work becomes something other than an unending
repetition or drudgery ? Can the future of
the technician be so secured and his daily
life so organized that his creative powers find
outlet as an integral part of a common purpose
thus encouraging his full development without
jeopardizing the position of his fellows in
society ? Upon the answer to these questions

much depends, including the future of the Trade Unions.

The history of the Trade Unions spreads into three centuries. They were born in the latter part of the eighteenth century. They grew throughout the nineteenth century from illegality to legality. Everyone admits the extraordinary part they have played in the history of this country and in the great social upheavals of this century.

There are also three great distinctive periods in the history of the unions. The Industrial Revolution of the latter half of the eighteenth century and the first third of the nineteenth century was the stormy generator of the Trade Unions. The revolution in the methods of production shattered the old domestic economy, completely transformed industry and agriculture, and created entirely new relations between the workers and the State, which from Elizabethan times had regulated the conditions of the workers in its typical feudalistic way. The impact of the new forces made such regulations incongruous and, whilst the masses were, historically speaking, driven forward, they carried with them all the traditions of the old economic regime. They smashed the machines and demanded state intervention and regulation of their conditions. They longed for the return of the past that could no longer be. The stage was set for the triumph of *laisser-faire* and the minimum of intervention in the affairs of industry.

The impossibility of the return to the past soon produced its reaction in the minds of the masses. They turned from the conservatism of their initial protests against the great changes in industry to become the visionary fighters for an entirely new system of society in which would be eliminated the social inequalities of the existing order and scope and power be given in co-operative industry to the toilers. What was a kind of civil war raged. The State had long since dropped what regulative role it had displayed. Now it ranged itself openly on the side of the rising capitalist class and stood over the masses as the new taskmaster of the employers in factory, mill, and mine.

It was in this period that Robert Owen talked of the " New Society coming like a thief in the night ", but workers like James Morrison would have none of the method of Owen who preached the transformation of society by rational appeals to the employers

and workers alike to combine. Morrison wanted
a Parliament in which all would be organized
on the basis of trades, but he was convinced
that the change would come only through the
class war, which he saw around him, being
carried to its logical conclusion. This was, of
course, a complete change from the outlook
of the machine smashers. The fight to return
to the past was replaced by the Utopian socialist
vision of the to-morrows.

The State, in the hands of the ruling class,
was used as a terrific weapon of class warfare
in defence of *laisser-faire* in industry in place
of the old Elizabethan protective laws regulating
wages, etc. This change is all important to
those who desire to appreciate the significance
of the age. Three-quarters of a century had
to pass before the State again pursued the
policy of " interference " in the administration
of industry. These years constitute the hey-day
of *laisser-faire* and the governing class only
tardily granted concessions when pressed by
mass actions by the workers.

This period witnessed a complete change in
the outlook of the workers. After the first
revolutionary struggle for Utopia, they adapted
themselves to capitalism, eschewed revolutionary

actions. They had little whatever to do with revolutionary theory and built their organizations with a view to their becoming an integral part of the existing system. This was the period of prosperous developing capitalism, and, despite the crises which occurred with regular frequency, so complete was the adaptation of the workers to the system that for more than fifty years the capitalists succeeded in maintaining such control over the thoughts and ideas of the workers in the Trade Unions that they kept back the formation of the Labour Party which is the political reflex of the Trade Unions.

The beginning of the twentieth century marked the beginning of new tendencies. The age of modern imperialist rivalries and crises had really begun. Britain and Germany were rushing headlong to Armageddon. The real wages of the workers of England began to fall. The class struggle sharpened. The Trade Unions stepped into the political arena with their Labour Representation Committees. The break with the old parties of capitalism had begun. A few years' rapid progress, culminating in the return of twenty-six Labour members to Parliament in 1906, called forth the great manœuvre of the Liberals led by Mr. Lloyd George in his famous Limehouse speeches. The speeches were followed by actions which signalled the beginnings of a new relationship of the State to the Trade Unions.

The State Insurance Act was the most important measure of the period. It was not merely a piece of social legislation conceding claims of a long standing character. It also changed the relation of the State to the Trade Unions. The unions were drawn closer to the State by the ingenious means of giving them a share in the administration of the State insurance funds.

At one stroke the State reappears in its role of the period prior to the Industrial Revolution. The Trade Boards for the regulation of conditions were a step in the same direction, though not so important, in that the apparatus of the unions was not so completely involved in collaboration with the State.

The State assumed a new importance to the unions. State Socialist ideas spread like wildfire. The demand for the nationalization of this and that industry became popular. The State was forced to interfere in industrial disputes partly as conciliator and regulator though always as the custodian of property interests. The questions of ownership and control became principal questions.

The question of the relation of the workers' organization to the State had thus reappeared after a century in an entirely new setting. In the opening period of the Industrial Revolution the workers' revolt against the machine and new forms and conditions of industry began by a pathetic desire to move backwards to a past that could not return. As soon as they recognized the impossibility of such an aim being realized, they, under the pressure of the crises following the Napoleonic wars, plunged into revolutionary struggles and set themselves revolutionary aims. Is the new relationship of the State to the workers' organizations inaugurated in the dawn of the twentieth century but the harbinger of a new revolutionary period ?

It may be argued that just as the crises following the Napoleonic wars were ultimately followed by a period of restoration and expansion so the War of the twentieth century, though followed by crises, will also be followed by prosperity and expansion. Such a reading of history will not bear examination.

Just as the new relation of forces between the workers and the State of the twentieth century differs from that of the beginning of the nineteenth century, in that the latter had to face the issue of a reversion to the past while the twentieth century issue is that of " ownership and control ", so also are the world economic relations different to-day from those of yesterday. After the Napoleonic wars there were hemispheres of economic development untapped. The possibilities of expansion were immeasurable. Modern capitalism had yet to spread its tentacles across the world.

The Trade Unions of the nineteenth century in the period of capitalist expansion could set funds aside to assist their members to emigrate and make hard and fast rules as to the number of apprentices to be employed in certain industries at one time. To-day emigration funds have not only vanished from the Trade Unions but no modern State would do other than make a laughing stock of itself were it to propound emigration as a cure for unemployment. There are no new hemispheres to be discovered and developed ; on the contrary, the world is completely discovered and portioned out amongst the big powers. The relation of the forces of production to the market capacity of the world is now one of contrast. The productive powers have enormously increased. Vast quantities of goods remain unpurchased and a huge army of thirty million unemployed walk the streets of the industrialized countries whilst uncounted millions of desolated peasantry of India and China add their tragic lot to the world's chaotic condition.

The Napoleonic wars were the product of the youth of capitalism in Europe. The World War of 1914–18 was the first great war of capitalism passed its zenith. It has not merely exhausted itself for a generation ; its frontiers are shattered, and the new economy of Socialism has firmly established itself over a sixth part of the earth inhabited by 160,000,000 people. The Utopias of the early Trade Unionists of the nineteenth century, of Owen and Morrison and others, are replaced by a reality of achievement in which the Trade Unions play an entirely new part which can be examined and tested in the light of experience. Instead of a reconstruction of the old world, it would appear that the old world is passing and the new is already born.

Is, then, the modern relationship of the

Trade Unions and the State in this country but a prelude to further changes more profound because more realistic and revolutionary? If there can be no new prosperous period for capitalism such as superseded the crises following the Napoleonic wars, must not the present compromising relations sooner or later end in the demand for a new order based on the principles already proved workable?

I am of the opinion that this is the case irrespective of the possible temporary victory of Fascism. For Fascism to triumph here would be a tragedy of immeasurable dimension, the restoration of the Dark Ages in twentieth century garb and blacker because of its modernity. But Fascism establishes no new principles of economy. It is a form of capitalism and not something which supersedes it. It establishes no new property relations. It aims only at putting the old ones in a strait-jacket.

Whatever is economically unsound must sooner or later perish, especially sooner rather than later when it becomes a matter of life or death for the great majority of mankind. And that is the issue before the capitalist world to-day whether or no it has the Fascist form. Fascism has nowhere solved the economic problems of capitalism. On the contrary, each day that goes by shows more clearly than before that Fascism is nothing other than the characteristic form of a stage of capitalist decline deeper than we have yet reached in this country, a stage wherein capitalism can continue only on the basis of the most violent repression of all the social and political elements and organizations either opposed to capitalism or merely favouring the liberal regime of capitalism's more prosperous period.

Yet it is the main body of this opposition to Fascism, namely the working class, upon which capitalism depends. To eliminate this class from capitalism is impossible. It is its life blood, the source of its profits and its power. Hence whatever the form of capitalism to-day, it is totally unable to remove the conditions which give rise to the Trade Unions and other forms of workers' organizations, because those conditions are inseparable from its own existence. Therefore although Fascism may destroy the existing Trade Unions, the struggle to destroy Fascism which would follow must of necessity give rise to the reappearance of Trade Unions.

They arose in all their varying forms as the instruments or weapons of the propertyless class against the class owning the means of production. So long as this property relation exists and governs the productive process the organized struggle of the property-less class against its exploitation cannot be eliminated.

The Trade Unions were the simplest and most elementary form of workers' organizations. Their forms were intimately related to the particular " vocation " of the workers especially when the " vocations " were much more clearly defined and separated than they are to-day. But it was not the vocation which determined the existence of the unions but the property or class relations. Had the vocation been the determining element in the situation then there would have been weaving and spinning craft unions in the period of " domestic economy " which preceded the Industrial Revolution. These unions, however, appeared after the Industrial Revolution and not before. They appeared in the textile industries first because the new property relations characteristic of modern capitalism found their sharpest expression in these industries.

Again, the unions were in the first place largely local, because of the geographical distribution of the industries and the absence of rail transport. When inventions made easier the lines of communication between town and town, the way was paved towards national organizations.

Yet again when the struggles of the unions repeatedly merged into class action against both the employers and the State the unions massed themselves together locally into Trades Councils and nationally into great Federations and into the Trades Union Congress.

The first indications of a recognition of the relation of the Trade Unions to the productive process and the possibility of their having to assume responsibility for the control of industry in the form of a " Parliament of Trades " belongs, as we have seen, to the period of revolutionary crises following the Napoleonic wars. It is not until the new revolutionary period of the twentieth century arrives that the idea emerges again in varying degrees of sharpness and clarity.

By the year 1910, syndicalist ideas were rampant throughout the Trade Union Movement. The shop stewards of the war period forced the question of " workers' control of industry " into the foreground of Trade Union thought and, by 1920, Mr. and Mrs. Webb modified their original attitude on the question and wrote " we ourselves look for the admission of nominees of the manual workers, as well as the technicians, upon the executive boards and committees, on terms of complete equality with other members in all publicly owned industries and services ; not merely, or even mainly, for the sake of the advantages of the counsel and criticism that the newcomers may bring from new standpoints, but principally for the sake of both inspiring and satisfying the increasing sense of corporate self-consciousness and public spirit among all those employed in these enterprises."

Thus the new revolutionary period has again thrown the question of property relations into the foreground of events. For the " control of industry " is inseparable from ownership. It arises as a demand from the resistance to exploitation and the attempts to modify it. It is not a far step from challenging particular conditions and terms of labour to the demand for the complete control of industry, especially when the competitive relations of capitalism intensify the exploitation of the workers at every stage of the productive process.

It must be remembered that the Trade Unions are organizations of workers *at work.* All the issues focused by the Trade Unions are bound up with the question of the terms upon which the work has to be done in thousands of different occupations. These terms are essentially property questions, expressing themselves in struggles between opposing classes for the products of industry. The more they multiply and become general, the more the control of the terms of labour, such as wages, hours of labour, conditions of work, give rise to the demand for the " control of industry " by the workers themselves.

To raise the issue of self-government in industry by those engaged in it, i.e. the control of the most vital phases of human activity, is to raise the revolutionary issue of a complete change of ownership. For ownership and control go together. " He who owns the means whereby I live, owns me " said Shakespeare long ago ; and it is just as true to-day. Ownership and control cannot be separated from each other. They who own industry control it. Hence the question of the " workers' control of industry " and the coming of the classless society based upon community ownership are inseparable questions also. They are therefore revolutionary issues and the Trade Unions are so intimately connected with them that a study of them and their readiness for their future tasks is imperative.

Chapter II

THE STRUCTURE OF THE
TRADE UNIONS

BEFORE discussing further any of the problems before the Trade Unions, it is
necessary to devote some attention to their
structure and how they work.

The unit of the Trade Union organization is,
of course, the branch. It is of importance to
recognize that in the great majority of cases the
Trade Union branch is based more on where
the workers live than on where they work.
There are a few cases where the branch is
based on the industrial principle, but only a
few, for example the tin-plate workers, bus-
men, and tramwaymen, form their branches
with the workshop, the garage, and depot as the
unit of organization.

The question of the relation of the branch to
the factory is a very important factor in the
life of the workers and their Trade Unions. The
unions in some industries approximate more

closely to the structure of the industry than in others, even though the residential principle of organization is maintained in relation to the branch. The miners' lodge, for example, approximates very closely to the pit membership. In some cases, all the workers of one pit are members of the same lodge. This, of course, is a considerable advantage from the standpoint of the familiarity of the members with each other and their direct acquaintance with the local problems.

But the average Trade Union branch is of the other kind. Hence it may have members scattered about in a score of factories, but because they live in a particular district they are members of a particular branch, all other factors of qualification being equal.

Many Trade Unionists believe that the residential branch has special advantages in that the members feel " safer ", i.e. farther away from the influence of the employers. At the same time it is considered more convenient because many live a considerable distance from their place of employment and do not want either to delay going home after work on the night of the branch meeting, or to have to travel home and then back again to the meeting.

There is considerable force in these arguments. But it must be admitted that such a unit of organization is only workable just so long as the branch has very limited functions. It can deal fairly adequately with unemployment benefit, sick benefit, and superannuation, collect contributions and report industrial grievances to a higher authority. But even with regard to these matters, the inadequacy of the present structure has been felt for many years.

This sense of inadequacy is clearly shown in the spread of the " shop steward " principle in the unions. The shop steward is a representative of the union " on the job ". In many cases he collects contributions, acts as spokesman of the workers with regard to grievances, keeps a watchful eye on the newcomers into the shop, examines the members' contribution cards, looks out for any violation of the customs and practices of the trade, and is an ever-present recruiting agent of the union.

The more active the Trade Unionists in the factories, the greater the difficulties of the residential branch become, and the greater the advantages of the industrial unit.

Let us see the average Trade Union branch at work. It meets, say, once a fortnight. It receives the contributions of its members, approves certain benefits being paid, listens to correspondence being read and discusses its contents, hears the reports of its representatives on the district committee and Trades Council and Labour Party. Members come along with proposition forms for new members. Others have " cases " to report concerning conditions in their factory, mill, or mine, etc. The complaints are sent forward to some higher authority in the organization. At best another fortnight must elapse before the branch learns of the result. It may be that there is delay owing to the district committee of the union having to call before it a deputation of the workers and the shop steward from the factory in which the grievance arose. It may then send the district secretary or organizer to interview the firm. Failing a settlement of the issue by such a visit, the matter must then pass to a local conference between the employers and the Trade Union representatives.

It is only necessary to multiply such incidents to realize how cumbersome and inadequate is the Trade Union machinery even with regard to its ordinary business arising from its bargaining position with the employers.

This was self-evident in the war-time experience of the shop stewards, who set the pace
throughout the Trade Union movement towards
the development of Trade Union factory organization. With the elimination of unemployment
by means of the mass slaughter on the battlefields of Europe, the transformation of all
industry into war industry, and the shattering
of old customs and practices by means of the
" dilution of labour ", the impetus was given to
direct action in the factories. The countless
reports to the Trade Union branches by their
members simply overwhelmed them. The
deluge of complaints concerning encroachments
on old customs, violation of agreements, etc.,
was too much for the normal machinery of the
unions. Nothing could cope with the situation
other than direct action and organization inside
the factory. The factory became the unit for
action on all the issues of struggle although the
old branches remained to deal with contributions and benefits of their social insurance.

The moment we consider the question of
" workers' control " of the productive process
the complete inadequacy of the present unit of
Trade Union organization must be at once
apparent. It would be impossible for the

workers of a factory, a mill, or a pit, to control their daily work by means of scattering themselves in a series of fortnightly meetings of two or three hours' duration. For the workers to control industry in an administrative sense, whatever meetings are necessary must be meetings of the workers of each factory and the representatives of the workers must be available " on the job ", which is an *everyday* job and not merely a fortnightly incident. For example, the question of the distribution of work in a factory could not wait for a fortnightly branch meeting. Nor could the consideration of a plan of work for a particular factory be dealt with by a branch composed of workers of a variety of factories. The plan for a factory could only be effectively considered by the workers of that factory who manned the machines and all the phases of the production process dealt with in the factory.

Hence the present unit of Trade Union organization is not merely weak from the standpoint of organizing the most effective collective action in defence of conditions, but it is totally unfitted for the larger purpose of " workers' control of industry ". Nevertheless, the massed power of the Trade Unions must not be underestimated. The consciousness that behind the individual unions there is the larger force of Trade Unionism as a whole, affects both employers and the non-organized mass of workers. It is this fact, supported by the experience of gigantic conflicts, that is the strength of the many agreements which exist to-day, governing the conditions of millions of workers.

The most important bodies above the branches are the district committees. These are composed of representatives of the branches of the district. As a rule they have little to do with the social insurance side of the work of the unions and deal more with the questions of policy in relation to wages, hours of labour, etc., and the observance of the local and national agreements established in conferences between the unions and the employers. A constant stream of communications pass to the district committees from the branches. Often in addition to the reports of the branch delegates they have before them the reports of the shop stewards.

The most important and authoritative body in the union is the executive council. Usually it is elected by ballot vote of the whole membership, sometimes by vote of the national conference of the union. Many executive councils are composed of full time members, but in a number of unions only one or two of the leading officials are so fully employed, while the executive members continue working at their trades. Upon this body depend all leading decisions of the unions, checked, of course, sometimes by ballot vote, sometimes by specially convened conferences, and sometimes by what is called a " final appeal court " composed of men " working at the trade " who are specially elected by ballot vote of the entire membership of the union.

Very few unions feel they can stand alone and so are linked together with other unions for various forms of combined action. For example, the Engineering and Shipbuilding Federation consists of forty-seven unions in the industry ; the Miners' Federation of Great Britain is a federation of county associations of miners, and so on. There are corresponding local federations which, under the general national scales, make local agreements with employers' federations concerning local conditions of employment.

A most important local grouping is that of the Trades Councils. They had their origin very often in sympathetic strike action, in which the Trade Unions of varying industries rallied to the support of unions in local or national

disputes. They have played an exceedingly
important part in the history of all phases of the
Labour Movement. They were in being long
before the Trades Union Congress and were
in part responsible for the formation of this
national " Parliament of the Trade Unions ".
At first they sent delegates to the Trades Union
Congress but on the plea that they involved dual
representation of union membership, the national
controllers of the unions succeeded by means of
their block votes in disaffiliating the Trades
Councils. For many years after they led an
existence independent of the Trades Union
Congress and formed a National Federation of
Trades Councils, but when in recent years
they again became the centres of considerable
militant activity, the Trades Union Congress
General Council succeeded, partly through the
antics of the Communist Party and partly
through the operation of the Trade Union Act
of 1927, in securing a very large measure of
control over them.

In addition to being the means of increasing
the solidarity of the unions, the Trades Councils
were the pioneers of political representation.
The famous " Junta " of the London Trades
Council in the 'sixties played an enormous part

in advancing the cause of independent labour representation in Parliament and thus paved the way to the formation of the Labour Party. So closely identified indeed were the Trades Councils with this political activity that, with the development of the Labour Party, many of them became Trades and Labour Councils, concerning themselves with both the industrial and political activity of the unions.

It was hoped by many that their political activity would supersede entirely their industrial activity. But these hopes were never really fulfilled. They did, however, contribute largely to a merging of industrial and political action, and often they became centres of great mass action on the part of the workers. They were, for example, the basis of the great convention of 1917 held in Leeds when Mr. Ramsay MacDonald, Lord Snowden, and the late W. C. Anderson, M.P., made speeches in favour of the formation of " Workers and Soldiers Councils " for Britain. They were the strength of the " Councils of Action " formed in 1920 with a view to calling a general strike to stop the war on Russia. In the General Strike of 1926, the local unity of the strike was centred in the Trades Councils.

The 1927 Trade Union Act hit the Trades and Labour Councils very hard. First it forced the party and the unions apart by means of the " contracting-in " clause in place of the " contracting out " clause. This meant the separation of the Labour Party from the Trades Councils. Secondly, the act hit at the sympathetic strike and especially the general strike.   It thus struck a heavy blow at the industrial activities of the Trades Councils which by virtue of their general class character tend to encourage working class unity as against the sectional interests.

The General Council of the Trades Union Congress were in the same period fearful of the influence of the Communist Party activities and put the Trade Unions into a strait-jacket by subjecting the Trades Councils to the discipline of the Trade Union executives. The Trades Union Congress bound the Trades Councils by a famous document declaring loyalty of the councils to the Trades Union Congress in which they had no representation. In addition it took charge of the national conferences which had hitherto been independent and replaced the independent executive of the Federation of Trades Councils with a Joint

Committee on which an equal number of the nationally elected representatives of the Trades Councils sit with representatives of the General Council of the Trades Union Congress.

The change thus accomplished was due in part to the vacillations of the Communist Party which at first stood for the independence of the Trades Councils. The General Council of the Trades Union Congress issued a document which insisted that the Trades Councils should accept the overruling authority of the Trades Union Congress and refuse association with other bodies who were outside that discipline. Many Trades Councils refused, when suddenly the Communist Party and the Minority Movement changed their minds and supported the General Council of the Trades Union Congress. This demoralized the resistance and the fight was lost.

To-day there is a high degree of centralization in the Trades Union Movement. All the local organizations I have enumerated are subject in some form or other to the discipline of the Trades Union Congress and the Trade Union Executives. The Trades Union Congress is, on matters of general policy, the highest authority of the Trades Union Movement. It meets

annually, but the General Council of the
Congress has the power to call special congresses
according to circumstance. The Congress is
composed of delegates from the Trade Unions
only. The number of delegates from each union
is proportionate to membership. In the Congress each union votes as a unit, although
minority views are usually permitted expression.
This form of block voting is the source of
much discontent and criticism, in that it is not
always a true reflex of the opinion of the union
delegation. Each union delegation has its own
meeting at the Congress at which it decides
how the union shall vote.

Hence an opinion in a delegation may be
defeated by one vote and result in the total
vote of the union, may be half a million votes,
being given in the opposite direction in the
Congress. A very false impression of the real
state of opinion in the Congress is frequently
given by the final votes cast on an issue.

The most important organ of the Congress
is the General Council which has very wide
powers. It consists of thirty-two members and
is elected annually by the Congress. For purposes of election the unions are grouped into
eighteen trade groups. For example, the unions

in the railway group are entitled to a certain proportion of representatives on the Council. The nominations for these positions are restricted to these unions, but the whole Congress votes on the nominations if there are nominated more than the specified number of candidates required.

The General Council is a post-War development in British Trade Unionism. It was first formed in 1922, following on the failure of the triple alliance of the railway, transport, and miners' unions. It was heralded as the " New General Staff " of the Trade Union Movement. Prior to its formation the Congress had been a very loose body indeed. Its central committee was nothing more than a Parliamentary Committee which made representation to Parliament on the matters discussed by Congress.

It was the absence of a centralized authority in Trade Unionism, when it was sorely needed in the big industrial disputes of 1911–12–13, that gave rise to such organizations as the triple alliance and projects for a quadruple alliance. The huge strikes and lock-outs of the early post-War years and the demand for greater working-class unity in the struggles forced the question of central leadership again into the foreground.

The great testing time for the new Council came in the General Strike of 1926, when it revealed both the limitations and the powers at its disposal. This is not the place to discuss the causes of the defeat of the General Strike. Such causes as there were must be sought in the policy pursued rather than in the mechanism of the unions.

The General Council has not the power to call a general strike, nor has the Trades Union Congress. Both may express themselves in favour of such but to give effect to any decision or view of the Congress, it must receive the authoritative backing of the Trade Union executives. The General Council of the Trades Union Congress may call a conference of the executives for such a purpose. Herein lies its power. This it did in 1926. Until there is a reorganization of the Trade Unions into industrial unions and a centralized body created to co-ordinate executive work, there is no other procedure open to the Trade Unions in such circumstances unless the unions voluntarily surrender their independence to the Trades Union Congress, a decision which would require an alteration in the constitution of each union. To secure such an alteration would be a long and tedious process.

Nevertheless, the General Council has great power to co-ordinate industrial action, to promote common action by the Trade Unions on general questions such as wages, hours of labour, to assist unions attacked on any vital question of Trade Union principle. It is under special instruction " in the event of there being a danger of an outbreak of war " to " call a special congress to decide on industrial action ". Besides these powers in relation to industrial action, it may initiate legislation as Congress may direct, levy the Trade Unions to pursue where necessary the legal interests of the Trade Unions with legal counsel in the House of Lords, interfere in inter-Trade Union disputes, maintain international Trade Union relations and conduct wide campaigns of propaganda in support of these objects.

It is this body with these wide powers which on behalf of the Trade Unions co-operates with the Executive of the Labour Party and the Central Council of the Co-operative Union in common political activities. How the whole Trade Union apparatus participates in the Labour Party, indeed provides the wide basis of the party, I will show later. Sufficient for the moment here to make clear the relationship of the central body of the Trade Unions to the Party as a separate organization. The General Council of the Congress, the Executive Committee of the Party and the leaders of the Parliamentary Labour Party hold joint sessions and issue from time to time agreed pronouncements on political questions affecting the whole Labour Movement.

Hence, although the Trade Union structure appears to be a mass of conflicting redundant bodies, it is really a highly centralized and disciplined body, exercising an enormous influence on the whole working-class movement.

CHAPTER III

THE FUNCTIONS OF THE
TRADE UNIONS

FOR what purpose does all this machinery and organized power exist ?

The first thing which must be strikingly clear to anyone who has given any study to Trade Unionism is the proletarian character of the movement. It is a movement of wage-workers. All its problems are based upon the fact that the members of the unions are wage-workers who, to live, must sell their labour power to the private owners of the means of production. They are parts of a competitive system, the motive of which is that of production for profit. The labour it uses is a commodity subject to all the laws of commodity production. The fundamental purpose of the Trade Unions, therefore, must be the pursuit of the interests of the wage-workers.

That their struggle takes on a defensive form at one stage and a revolutionary form at another is due entirely to the relations existing between the class forces at a particular time. This relationship depends basicly upon the economic maturity and stability of the system—both in part and as a whole.

It must be realized, however, that the revolutionary significance of any action, whether it be political or of a direct mass type, does not depend entirely upon what the participants think of it. This depends upon the relation of the classes at the time and whether it changes that relationship in the direction of the abolition of classes.

For example, the General Strike of 1926 was not undertaken with a view to overthrowing the existing system, but it profoundly shook the system and contributed in no small degree to the subsequent tremendous increase of the Labour vote in 1929, aiming at Socialism as against capitalism. Indeed it must be recognized that viewed objectively the marshalling of the forces of labour under the banner of Socialism for the purpose of achieving political power to abolish capitalism, in this period of chronic crisis of capitalism, is revolutionary. It is the failure to recognize this fact and consciously to direct the whole policy of the Trade Unions and the Labour Movement in the light of that recognition that constitutes the greatest danger facing the coming Labour government, threatening the movement with disintegration and the triumph of counter-revolution in the form of Fascism.

The transition from one system to another is by no means a mechanical process. However " inevitable " the change may be, the time necessary to effect it can never be measured. Nor can the amount of human suffering and conflict involved before the change is carried through be estimated. So uncertain is the " inevitability " that the possibility of a period of blackest reaction and disintegration of civilization cannot be ruled out of the perspectives of capitalist society.

Everything in this respect depends upon the development of the socialist ideas in the ranks of the people and the growth of the will to power on the part of the Labour forces for the purpose of Socialism, before the forces of reaction are able to consolidate their power under the banner of Fascism. This fateful issue was presented to the Labour Movement in each country where Fascism to-day holds power prior to the victory of Fascism. Had the Labour and Socialist Movement of Italy seized the opportunity presented to it in the fateful days of 1921, when the workers took control of the factories, and consolidated that victory by conquering the powers of the State, Fascism in Italy would have been defeated in its infancy.

Had the German Labour Party in 1918, when the power of the State fell into its hands after the fall of the Kaiser, advanced decisively to the fulfilment of its socialist aims, instead of concentrating upon formal democracy and leaving the economic power in the hands of the landlords and capitalists as heretofore, Hitlerism could never have flourished. Fascist ideas spread amongst the masses proportionately to their disillusionment with a Labour Movement which has failed to grasp its historic opportunity to fulfil its socialist aims.

Hence the importance of evaluating the work and functions of the Trade Unions correctly in relation to their fundamental aims and those of the whole Labour Movement. That the Trade Unions are committed to socialist aims is not a matter for debate. They are committed to it by virtue of their relation to the Labour Party, by the Trade Union Congress constitution and its decisions. The stated objects of the

Trades Union Congress put the "nationalization of the land, mines and minerals, and railways " in the forefront of its demands and aims. The most recent Congress (1934) re-affirmed " Our complete faith in the principles of Socialism ".

Therefore when discussing the functions of the unions in relation to industry it must never be forgotten that they are also waging a political struggle with and through the Labour Party. The deeper the crisis of the present system grows, the more the question of political power assumes an importance to which all other questions become subordinate and the more the fundamental aims supersede the incidental. As a matter of fact the latter merge into the former and become unrealizable unless the basic changes are achieved.

Of the bearing of this question on the future of the unions it will be necessary to discuss. Here let us turn to what are usually called the specifically Trade Union functions of this powerful machine whose structure I have sketched.

These can be divided into two, namely those of social insurance and those dealing with the conditions of employment. Long before the days of State Insurance and the Old Age Pensions

Act the Trade Unions provided insurance against sickness, injury, old age, and unemployment. The administration of these funds was supplemented in every Trade Union branch by innumerable spontaneous acts of assistance to members who had exhausted benefits, or who through some misfortune had failed to qualify for benefit. These benefits have been maintained since the coming of State Insurance and have contributed considerably to the amelioration of the conditions of millions of workers in the critical years since the War.

The social insurance aspect of Trade Unionism gives a vested interest to the members and is an important factor in the stability of the unions. The social life of the Trade Union branch is reinforced by the Trade Union social clubs, in which members and friends foregather fraternally and thereby consolidate the social bonds of their class.

The industrial side of Trade Union activity is most extensive. The unions regulate wages, hours of labour, etc., by means of collective agreements with the employers. In some industries, where the workers are well organized, the unions have agreements covering the employment of labour, the regulation of overtime, protective safety regulations, etc. The miners have their independent checkweighmen who check the weight of coals sent up from the pit. They are also entitled by statute to appoint examiners to inspect the pit. The builders have codes of safety regulations. The Transport and General Workers Union have many agreements governing allocations of work schedules, de-casualization schemes for workers, etc. Probably the largest field of influence is that of the unwritten rules and customs. These extend in many directions, such as the distribution of work, overtime regulations, starting and stopping times for meals, the introduction of new machinery, the transfer of labour, limitations and training of apprentices, outworking allowances, etc.

In this century there has been a considerable extension of joint action with the State. One of the most important is the Trade Board system, through which the employers throughout the industries concerned are compelled to observe minimum wage standards. The Trade Boards are established in industries where the workers are badly organized. The conditions of the workers in what are known as the " sweated industries " gave rise to them. The Boards are comprised of equal numbers of employers' and workers' representatives, together with " independent " members appointed by the Minister of Labour. One of the most important of these is the Agricultural Wages Board.

In some industries there are what is known as Whitley Councils, a system of Joint Industrial Councils launched by the Government immediately after the war as a counter move to the independent workers' committees of the shop stewards. The latter were demanding an increasing share in the control of industry as the means to social ownership. The Government answered with the scheme of equal representation of the employers and workmen in factory committees and national and local industrial councils to maintain private ownership. These councils were to be held responsible for discussing the general state and policy of industry and the efficiency of its administration. It meant that the workers' organizations had to become a kind of efficiency bureau for the employers. In most cases where they were established they became in practice concerned mainly with questions of wages and hours.

A further development of conciliation machinery arose from the pressure of the workers' organizations for improvement of conditions, in the form of conciliation boards and tribunals. These, of course, can work just so long as the employers and the Government are in a position to make concessions to the economic demands of the workers. But as soon as the pressure of the crisis conditions of capitalism tend to prohibit such concessions, the arbitration and conciliation machinery breaks down. The experience of the Railway Wages Board is a case in point. So long as it had a basis for compromise decisions there was no question of it being discarded. When the wages question became acute and the unions refused to concede further to the employers, the latter proposed the abolition of the Wages Boards and the establishment of a legal arbitrator whose decision would be final and legally binding.

The intensification of the competitive struggle in a number of industries has been accompanied by an ignoring of agreements between employers and the Trade Unions. From this state of affairs has come the demand for the legalizing of agreements and arbitration awards. This has appeared in the cotton and iron and steel industries and represents a dangerous innovation in which the workers and their organizations will be brought under the direct control of the State.

Besides these forms of arbitration machinery for holding the Trade Unions back from the path of direct mass action on economic questions such as wages and hours of labour, the unions have their representatives in a variety of Government created advisory committees such as the National Advisory Council for Juvenile Unemployment, Courts of Referees for dealing with appeal cases in the administration of the State Unemployment Insurance.

A further important development in the direction of collaboration with the employers and the Government took place after the General Strike of 1926. The General Council of the Trades Union Congress and subsequently almost all the Trade Union executives appeared to abandon the idea of ever again using the strike weapon. Although the Government and leading employers had used the most threatening language to the unions and had passed the Trade Union Act of 1927, which literally hamstrung the unions, the General Council of the Trades Union Congress, with the approval of the unions, entered into entirely new relations with the employers through the Federation of British Industries and the Confederation of employers. They mutually agreed to issue joint statements on such subjects as Unemployment, Industry and Finance, Social Service, Empire Development, and kindred subjects all on the basis of the restoration of capitalism, and entirely remote from the declared aims of the Trade Union Congress and the Labour Party. They issued a joint memorandum on Finance to the World Economic Conference of 1932, which the Conservative Chancellor of the Exchequer welcomed as a document which he could himself have drafted with satisfaction. Later the General Council sent representatives to the Empire Conference at Ottawa convened by the British Government.

All these forms of working with the State and the employers have grown out of the function of the unions, in acting as a brake upon the intensive exploitation of the workers. The basis of this superstructure of conciliation is the strike weapon, i.e. the organized power of the workers to withhold their labour. Despite the obvious deviation from the declared socialist aim, and the conscious effort on the part of the unions to " make capitalism work " and condition their demands to the "balance sheets" of capitalism, the unions have repeatedly found themselves in the position of direct opposition to the State and the employers. The General Strike of 1926 is, of course, the classic incident illustrating the logic of the economic contradictions between the claims of the workers and the capitalists.

It may be said that this occurred before the new plans for co-operation were established. Such a plea cannot be made concerning the actions of the unions in 1931. Their unanimous resistance to the " economy demands " brought down the Labour Government.

The main function of the unions, therefore, is the pursuit of the interests of the working-class. The defence of its interests accentuates the crisis of capitalism, as was demonstrated in 1926 and 1931. The apparent rise in status which appeared to be emerging with the growth of collaboration with the State and the employers proves to be false in the face of the intensified exploitation of the workers. There is no increase of responsibility for production, no change in the wage-slave position of the workers. Such changes can come only with the change in ownership of the means of production.

Thus the defence of the economic interests of the workers and the question of their status merges into a single issue—the achievement of the fundamental aims of the Labour Movement —as the means of solving the immediate " bread and butter " questions which occupy the continual attention of the Trade Unions.

CHAPTER IV

THE TRADE UNIONS AND THE STATE

THERE have been many words written and many disputations concerning the nature of the State. Some people confuse the term State with Society, and regard them as synonymous. Actually the State arose with the institution of private property and became the authority of propertied interests over society in the name of society.

Theoretically it is supposed to be impartial and to hold the balance between the conflicting interests of the propertied and non-propertied elements in society. Actually it governs society in the interests of property and can do no other. The moment a State comes into being which does otherwise it must be the instrument of a social revolution in opposition to private property, abolishing private property and therefore the basis of its own authority over society. The new basis of community or social ownership paves the way to the administration of

things as distinct from the government of people
in the interests of classes. Then, and then only,
will it be possible to organize society according
to social functions performed.

From the moment the Trade Unions came
into existence they found themselves in opposition to the State. The Industrial Revolution,
to which I have already referred as the generator
of modern capitalism, changed the policy of
the State. For more than a century of the
development of mercantile capitalism, the State
had carried on many of the old Elizabethan
practices of regulating workmen's conditions
by legislation and agreements between the
justices of the peace and the merchant guilds
of the towns. The Industrial Revolution
shattered these old practices just as it shattered
the domestic economy of Feudalism. All
stability of conditions vanished. The new
inventions ploughed up the old conditions with
machines.

The State did not rush to the rescue of the
new proletariat. On the contrary it drove them
into the factories and unleashed a terror such
as had not been seen in the history of the country.

The workers did not understand the significance of the Industrial Revolution. They simply

E

knew that some new force was battering down the old conditions, breaking up their homes, driving them into the factories, hounding them from place to place. They longed for the serenity of the order that had been destroyed, for old customs that had been their life. They saw in the machine an enemy. They began smashing the machines and appealing to the State to resume the old modes of settling differences.

The ruling classes viewed things differently. For them the old order had to go. Untold wealth lay before them in the new processes of production. They were alarmed also by the French Revolution and saw in every protest of the workers a conspiracy to overthrow the system. The King's Speech of 1st December, 1793, claimed that a desperate conspiracy was afoot to destroy the constitution and uproot law and order. The Habeas Corpus Act was suspended in 1794. The Treasonable Practices Acts were put through Parliament, destroying the right of free speech, printing, and writing; the Seditious Meetings Acts empowered any magistrate to break up a public meeting; stamp duties were imposed to increase the price of papers; a censorship was imposed on the printers; the Combination Acts declared all Trade Unions illegal. Political Societies were suppressed. Savage prosecutions were under- taken against radicals. No one reading the history of this period could question for a single moment that the State was the organ of class domination.

From the earliest days of Trade Unions to the beginning of the twentieth century, through- out the revolutionary period of the first forty years of the nineteenth century and the whole period of triumphant industrial capitalism which followed, the Trade Unions and the Labour Movement in its entirety had to fight their way against the State. Indeed, it is important to observe that it is not until the dawn of the twentieth century and the failure of the Liberal Party, under the leadership of Asquith and Lloyd George, to stem the advance of the Labour Movement as an independent force that there is a profound change in the attitude of the ruling class parties through the State to the Labour Movement.

That this change coincides with the beginning of the general crisis of the whole world of capitalism is significant in the extreme and in the writer's opinion has not been realized by the

Labour Movement. The historians have been so obsessed with narrating events in chronological order and so adaptable to capitalism itself, that this most fateful landmark in the political history of Britain has received little attention. Where it *has* been noticed then that notice has usually been for entirely opposite reasons to those which I wish here to emphasize.

It is obvious that up to 1825 the State was used in what proved to be an unavailing effort to wipe out the Trade Unions entirely. Through the great efforts of Francis Plaice and Joseph Hume the Combination Laws directed against the Trade Unions were repealed in 1824. Caught, as it were, unawares, the Government spent another year trying to re-fetter the unions. From this time forward to the end of the century, government after government continued the struggle to shackle the Trade Unions.

Mr. Milne-Bailey, in his book *Trade Unions and the State*, says, concerning the legal position of the Trade Unions in the nineteenth century : " The lack of uniformity and the uncertainty of the position illustrates clearly enough the fact that the State had not thought out its attitude to Trade Unionism. It had no clear idea as to the right relationship between Trade Unionism and the State, no underlying philosophy of the new industrial system and the function of the important institutions within it. The Trade Union Movement was equally devoid of such a philosophy."

What Mr. Bailey really means is that neither the ruling class nor the working class held his views concerning the relation of the unions to the State. For the ruling class of the last century proved by word and deed that they had very clear and definite ideas on this question. They regarded themselves as a ruling class and systematically and vigorously resisted every effort of the masses for the extension of the franchise. A veritable civil war had to be waged to secure the extension of the franchise in 1832. Eighty more years had to pass before the principal features of the Chartist programme of 1834 became law. The women of England had to wage the most violent struggle and be the victims of the most disgusting brutality before they won the vote.

The ruling class may have had a wrong philosophy from the point of view of Mr. Bailey —but they had a philosophy—of class domination in the interests of private property.

Nor was there any ambiguity in their view of the Trade Unions. They have regarded the unions consistently as the organs of a class enemy. The Combination Laws of 1799 greeted their inception. Twenty-five years of struggle had to take place before the Trade Unions were lawful. The whole history of the Trade Unions has been one long trail of economic and political victimization of Trade Unionists, the hampering of union development with fettering legislation. The Tolpuddle Martyrs, Peterloo and the crushing of the Chartist insurrectionaries, the Featherstone shootings, etc., all speak the language and philosophy of class war against the working class.

Up to 1871 the Trade Unions had no legal status although their existence was permissible. They had no property status. They could neither buy property nor sell it. They were subject to all the conspiracy laws. Even after the passing of the 1871 Trade Union Act the activities of the unions were strictly limited. The Master and Servants Act of 1874 had hardly arrived on the Statute book before the Criminal Law Amendment Act was passed. The former legalized strikes. The latter made illegal all efforts to make a strike a success. It is only necessary to add to these the Osborne and Taff Vale Judgments and finally the Trade Union Act of 1927 to demonstrate completely that, with regard to the Trade Unions also, the class war philosophy of the capitalist class in relation to the working class has never been wanting in clarity of formulation or decisiveness in practice.

The Trade Union Act of 1927 limited the scope of strike action, prohibited sympathetic strikes outside the limits of an industry, made political strikes illegal, severed the Trade Unions connected with State departments from the Trades Union Congress and the Labour Party, and struck at the political activities of the unions by the imposition of the " contracting-in clause ", hoping thereby to cripple the funds of the Labour Party.

It is not an exaggeration to say that whatever concessions have been won by the workers' organizations have been won through a century and a half of tremendous political and economic struggle.

It is also not true to say that " the Trade Union Movement was equally devoid of an underlying philosophy of the new industrial system and the functions of the important institutions within it ".   In the first decades of Trade Unionism, revolutionary theories held sway, visualizing the rapid transformation of the industrial system into a co-operative commonwealth, in which the Trade Unions and Co-operative Societies would function as the administrative machinery of the new society.

After the collapse of the Chartist Movement in the 'forties of the last century, with the beginning of the years of expanding capitalist development, the Trade Unions were dominated by the Liberal philosophy of *laisser faire*.

Mr. and Mrs. Webb referring to the passing of the 1871 Act quote the old Trade Unionists as saying, " The less working men have to do with the law in any shape the better." And that view was echoed by the Trades Union Congress of 1868 and the Trades Councils of Manchester and Birmingham in 1869.

The minority led by the famous " Junta " of the London Trades Council kept up a constant pressure for political changes and were responsible for the next big change in the law. The Employers' and Workmen's Act, 1874, changed matters considerably. The basis of collective bargaining was laid. This is seen in the memorial of official representatives of the Trade Unions to the Home Secretary in 1875. It says, " We do not seek to interfere with the free competition of the individual in the exercise of his craft in his own way ; but we do reserve to ourselves the right either to work for, or to refuse to work for, an employer according to the circumstances of the case, just as the master has the right to discharge a workman or workmen ; and we deny that the individual right is in any way interfered with when it is done in concert."

And always in the background stood the State as the dominant authority—over the workmen. It was on the basis of collective bargaining that the cumulative work of building the unions proceeded rapidly. But the State authorities were not befogged at all on the question of their relations to the unions. They knew what they wanted and why they wanted it. And, as a matter of fact, the material conditions for the presence of any other relationship than that which existed throughout this period up to the beginning of the twentieth century did not exist.

The Trade Unionists at this stage were saturated with the philosophy of Liberalism and neither wanted the State to interfere in industry

nor the Trade Unions to have anything to do
with the State.

On the other hand, there were other currents
of thought in the Trade Unions though they
were in a minority. These were the Marxists
of the First Workingmen's International, formed
in 1864, to which a number of the English
Unions were affiliated and the group of re-
formers concentrated in the London Trades
Council in the 'sixties. Both waged the fight for
independent political representation through
the formation of an independent Labour Party.
The Marxists held a definitely revolutionary
philosophy, and have always held a systematic
body of socialist opinion in relation to the
State, its character and functions. The re-
formers of the " Junta " of the London Trades
Council had a more limited philosophy and
estimate of the situation. They favoured the
democratization of the capitalist State, but did
not get beyond the fight for independent Labour
representation.

A further development of thought within
the whole Labour Movement took place in
the 'eighties with the formation of the Fabian
Society, the Independent Labour Party, the
Social Democratic Federation, etc., all of which

held definite views concerning the State and its evolution. True they were in a minority, but they undoubtedly played an enormous part in preparing the Trade Unions for the next stage of their political evolution with the turn of the century.

From the collapse of Chartism in the 'forties to the end of the nineteenth century, the Trade Unions had lived through the period of prosperous and apparently ever-expanding capitalism. It was the hey-day of Liberalism and the Trade Unions reflected that philosophy. Its concrete expression is " collective bargaining " between the unions and the employers.

The turning point in the development of the relations between the classes was reflected in the struggle for the change in the legal status of the Trade Unions. Outstanding in this struggle was the Trades Dispute Act of 1906 and the Trades Union Act of 1913. The first arose out of the famous Taff Vale Judgment of 1901 which held the Trade Unions collectively responsible for the actions of individual members in disputes. The sequel to this judgment was a tremendous impetus to the political fight for the formation of the Labour Party. The second arose out of the Osborne Judgment which was a challenge to the unions concerning the use of their funds for political purposes. The Government gave way and reversed the Osborne Judgment in the Trades Union Act of 1913, providing a " contracting-out " clause for those who objected to paying the political levy after a ballot of the union members had proved favourable.

These two Acts mark the turning point from one stage to another in the history of the relations of the Trade Unions to the State. The Taff Vale decision gave fresh inspiration to the campaign for independent political representation of Labour ; the Osborne Judgment was an attempt to put the brake on the political developments of Labour now well begun.

The first workers' party arose in the early revolutionary period that gave rise to the Chartist Movement. The Chartist Movement itself was a great working-class political movement with a reform programme for the extension of the franchise, etc. This movement was divided between those who thought of the programme only as a means of assisting the development of a revolutionary crisis in which power could be seized and an entirely new kind of society established, and those who regarded the reforms as the next stage in the social and political evolution of the country.

With the defeat of the Chartist Movement in 1842 and the passing of the economic crisis into prosperous industrial capitalism Labour politics were almost completely submerged until the end of the century. The coming of the new crisis in capitalism at the beginning of the twentieth century had the reverse effect. Independent Labour politics reappeared on the basis of a powerful mass Trade Union movement. This revolutionary fact, i.e. the appearance of a class as a conscious political force on the historical stage had two aspects. One was that it coincided with the change in economic relations of the powers internationally and a sharpening of class relations internally. The other was the new alignment of political forces.

Internationally the monopoly stage of capitalism had begun and the Great War loomed ahead, a fact which was recognized by every international labour conference. Internally the relations between the classes had become steadily more acute. Real wages were falling whilst the new attack upon the unions had awakened masses of workers to political consciousness. The beginning of the end of the Liberal Party had arrived.

No one has brought this point out with greater clarity than Mr. Lloyd George in his explanation of the significance of the Limehouse campaign. I have emphasized this elsewhere (*Preparing for Power*). I emphasize it again. Addressing the Liberals he said, " If a Liberal Government tackle the landlords, the brewers, and the peers, as they have faced the parsons and try to deliver the nation from the pernicious control of the confederacy of Monopolists, then the Independent Labour Party will call in vain upon the working men of Britain to desert Liberalism that is gallantly fighting to rid the land of the wrongs that have oppressed those who labour in it." (Beer's *History of British Socialism*, p. 349.)

A whole series of measures followed immediately, measures which signified both the new political relations between the classes and the parties and the new beginning of the new relations between the unions and the State. The most important of these Acts were : The Old Age Pensions Act of 1908, the Trades Boards Act of 1909, the National Insurance Act of 1911, the Coal Mines Act of 1912.

Up to this time the Trade Unions and the Friendly Societies had been the only bodies providing for old age and unemployment insurance. The State now became the principal custodian of these matters. This is important in itself as signifying a new attitude of the ruling class to the growing working class. But more important, however, is the machinery created by the Unemployment Insurance Act and the Trades Boards Act. Through this machinery the new stage of collaboration of the State and the Trade Unions begins. The Trades Unions became part of the administrative machinery of State Insurance. The Trades Boards formed the first machinery of collaboration between the State, the Trade Unions, and the Employers. The Mines Act of 1912 enacted a State settlement of a large industrial dispute and the establishment of a legal minimum wage for miners.

These measures have been welcomed by many as the triumph of liberal ideas in the State, signifying the ascent of the Trade Unions to a new status, foreshadowing the greater democratization of the State. That these measures conceded considerable amelioration of the workers' conditions cannot be disputed.

But it is necessary to give a different estimate concerning the future democratization of the State. Appearances are often deceptive and none more so than political appearances. In my judgment these changes are symptomatic of the development of a crisis in which the whole fabric of the capitalist State would be challenged. The concessions do not represent a growing friendliness between the classes but a manœuvre of classes preparing for battle, however much the leaders on both sides deplore the idea of class warfare. The alarm expressed by Mr. Lloyd George concerning the oncoming labour masses gives the key to the whole situation. The economic concessions were intended to appease the workers. The political changes in the relation of the State to the unions were an effort to embrace the unions with the tentacles of the State apparatus in order to smother their class struggle activity.

The deeper the crisis became the greater was the need of the capitalist class to secure the collaboration of the workers to save the system. Only a few years had to pass before this was demonstrated completely. The War clinched the matter in its entirety. Within a few months of the outbreak of war in 1914 the Trade Unions were locked in the tight embrace of the State. Throughout the War the Trade Unions functioned practically as departments of State. Labour Party and Trade Union leaders entered the Cabinet. Every department of State directly responsible for the running of industry was invaded by Trade Union representatives. The Defence of the Realm Act, the Munitions Act, and all the attendant mechanism of tribunals, arbitration, and the like, held the unions in a tight grip. All the patriotic feeling roused by the War, the fears, and social aspirations of the millions of people enveloped them. They became organs of the State for the prosecution of the War.

But this was founded on contradictions inherent in the private ownership of the means of production. The machine of State had become larger. Its powers of repression had grown enormously. Yet an internal transformation was taking place, because of the class contradictions, which, sooner or later, was bound to break the collaborative mechanism that had been erected.

Unemployment was abolished and wage-slavery remained. Dilution of labour broke down the old traditions and customs, but it also

F

drove all kinds of labour together, broadened and deepened the class struggle which soon broke through the restrictions, challenged the collaboration that had been established and burst into new forms of organized independent action, led by the shop stewards. War weariness played its part and then came the impact of revolution from Europe, the unleashing of the demands for the realization of the vast hopes that had been raised in the name of democracy.

Under the cover of the War and the new collaboration of the workers' organizations with the State, there had been a great advance in organized strength and a big political awakening. The Insurance Act, in particular, played a role which was not intended by its authors. It helped to sweep the workers into the unions in a period when the absence of unemployment gave a consciousness of strength such as they had not experienced before. Hence, with the termination of war, it could hardly be a matter of surprise that a great deal of the collaborative machinery broke down. The Labour and Trade Union representatives were drawn out of the Cabinet, though a residue of officials were left in Government departments.

There was an extension of the franchise. The unions were freed from direct State control.

A decade of class war opened such as had not been seen in the history of modern capitalism. In the first two years after the war the workers advanced to the attack. The capitalists retreated, granting big concessions in wages and hours of labour. Out of these first rounds of the conflict began a fresh stage in the development of State machinery, not for social peace, but for class war. The organized power of the workers had now reached its highest point and was growing rapidly. The Scottish forty hour strike, followed by the great railway strike of 1919, the threatened miners' stoppage, the desperate playing for time by the setting up of the Sankey Commission in relation to the mining industry, the cotton strike of six hundred thousand cotton workers, told the world clearly that there could be no going back to pre-War times.

The association of the workers with the State organizations for the prosecution of the War now had its reaction upon the minds of the workers. Having witnessed what the State could do for war they now expected it to use the same kind of drastic power for the transformation of social conditions in peace.

The mass struggles of this period thus became immediately a series of gigantic conflicts of the workers against the State, as the custodian of the interests of the employers. The capitalists at once set on foot the organization of machinery for strike-breaking. It reached its most complete form in the organization of the O.M.S. (Organization for the Maintenance of Supplies). In 1920 the Government of the day—a coalition of Tories and Liberals—passed the Emergency Powers Act for the purpose of enabling the State to assume ditatorial powers at any moment against the workers. It may be that the adaptation of the State for " emergency " may sometime turn against its authors, but at this stage it is important to observe that no such idea entered their heads at the time of the passing of this legislation and at no time has it been used against anyone other than the workers in disputes.

The Defence of the Realm Act had established a dictatorship for the war-time phase of the crisis of the system. Immediately the war had ended the economic and social crisis assumed larger proportions and the passing of the Emergency Powers Act was the first act of strengthening the powers of the State for social conflict.

This is regarded by some people as the first step in the direction of Fascism. It is doubtful whether this is so, although shortly afterwards Fascist organizations did make their appearance. At that time, however, Fascism had developed no coherent philosophy or forms of organization. It would be more correct to say, therefore, that it represented a characteristically panic action on the part of the ruling class, foreshadowing the crystallization of a more desperate yet more coherent policy of Fascism, that marks a later stage of the crisis of the system.

During the years of the mass attacks of the workers (1919–1920) a deluge of " Reconstruction Schemes " descended on the country, under which the State was to play a more paternal democratic role than ever before. The purpose of these schemes was clear enough. Shaw ends one of his plays with the expression, " Keep on talking Jack "—this might be appropriately applied to all these schemes and commissions. They had one purpose—to keep the Labour Movement talking until the waves of mass

action had exhausted themselves and the hour
for counter action had arrived.

The tide turned at the end of 1920 and early
in 1921 the counter attack was launched.
All capitalist enterprises were finally freed from
the war-time State control in order that the
system might become adapted to " peace "
production. At the same time the State took a
leading part in driving the workers into the
surrender of many of the gains secured in the
preceding years. This period culminated in
the General Strike of 1926, and the miners'
lock-out which preceded and followed it. The
Emergency Powers Act came into operation
along with the O.M.S.

The effect of this counter-offensive was far-
reaching. The Trades Union Act of 1927 added
new strength to the State against the workers.
It deprived the Trade Unions of important
powers. It split away the Trade Unions in the
Civil Service from the Trades Union Congress
and the Labour Party.   It struck at the political
rights of the Trade Unions along the lines of
the Osborne Judgment for the " contracting-
out " clause of the 1913 Trade Union Act was
repealed and replaced by a " contracting-in "
clause, designed to break the political solidarity

of the workers in the Trade Unions. Political strikes, i.e. strikes intended to coerce the State, were declared illegal. Sympathetic strikes of the workers of one industry with another were made illegal.

A comparison of the position of the relation of the Trade Unions to the State in 1914–18 with 1927 is illuminating. In the first period the Trade Unions were embraced by the State and given concessions in status and conditions, because British capitalism was challenged by rivals. From 1918–1927 the State, faced with an internal crisis, relentlessly fought the Trade Unions, stripped them of many economic gains, divided their forces, deprived them of powers, and fettered them with political restrictions.

Indeed it may be said that the ruling class of this country here began the process of consciously directing the evolution of the democratic State into the Corporate State of Fascism. From this time onward, they have pursued a consistent policy of strengthening the powers of the State, depleting political democracy, and fettering the forces of labour. The fierce class struggle between 1918–1927 had been waged without any marked encroachments on the political rights of the workers, and with the

exception of the " Emergency Powers Act ",
without any great changes in the structure of
the State.

The Trades Dispute Act of 1927 definitely
ended this phase of British history. It put a
stranglehold on strike action, struck at the
Labour Party—the political machinery of the
workers—and put the workers employed by
the State in a political category of their own,
half-way between that of the army and
civilians, but under the domination of the State.

The country had not long to wait for the
maturing of the policy. The economic crisis
did not abate—on the contrary it became more
acute. To the surprise of the Conservative
Government, the 1929 election demonstrated
that its attack on the funds of the Labour
Party had been overcome, and had not proved
effective enough to hold back the political
development of that Party. The Labour Party
formed the Government without having a
majority over the Tories and Liberals. It dared
neither to challenge capitalism nor to do other
than function as a hidden coalition government ;
its public name being a " Minority Labour
Government ". The catastrophic development
of the economic crisis provided the ruling class

with the opportunity to leap into the saddle of government by splitting the Labour Movement, under the banner of a " National Government " to " Save the Nation ".

How much the lack of political sense on the part of Messrs. MacDonald, Snowden, and Thomas was responsible it is difficult to say, but the fact remains that, although they called for the splitting of the Labour Party, they failed to take a single Labour organization with them, and were compelled to form a new body called National Labour. At the same time it was a terrific shock to the Labour Movement to lose three leaders of thirty years' standing, at the moment of being plunged into a General Election. More significant, however, is the evidence of the strength and loyalty of the working-class, in standing so firmly against the shock.

The election had many features of Fascist thought and practice, such as panicky stunts, nationalism, a bastard flag-wagging patriotism, the rousing of ignorant fears. Promptly after the return of the National Government, composed of an overwhelming number of Tories, split Liberals, and a small Labour cotery around Mr. MacDonald, it launched a

programme of economic nationalism, transformed the fiscal system of the country from
free trade to tariffs and quotas, started a
currency war, and developed an attack on the
economic standards of the workers. Unemployment benefits were cut, standards of relief
scaled down, wages and salaries were reduced.

But more significant still were the singular
measures adopted which distinguished the
Government's new attacks from the old. Their
singularity consists in the Government's
adoption of Fascist principles. Fascism,
Mussolini defines as " disciplined Capitalism ! "
All appointments are from above. Nobody is
elected. Everything is done by decree, whether
it be the fixing of prices or the forming of a
special corporation or the settling of a dispute.
Planned capitalism is the theme. Government
by decree is the method. Discipline in the
interests of the existing system is the objective.

Mr. MacDonald speaking to the National
Labour Committee on 6th November, 1933,
put the matter thus :—

> " The secret of the success of dictatorships
> is that they have somehow or other to make
> the soul of a nation alive. We may be shocked
> at what they are doing, but they have certainly

awakened something in the hearts of their people which has given them a new vision and a new energy to pursue national affairs. In this country the three parties in co-operation are doing that, and our task must be to get the young men with imagination, hope, and vision behind us."

The similarity of words is well supported by deeds. For example, under the Abnormal Importations Act the Board of Trade can, by order, with the concurrence of the Treasury, apply the Act to further imports if *they* are satisfied (not Parliament) that it is necessary.

Then came the Horticultural Products Act of 1931, which empowers the Minister of Agriculture and Fisheries to act in similar manner (without reference to Parliament). In 1932 the Import Duties Act set up another committee with similar powers. These have been followed by the notorious agricultural policy of Mr. Elliott which consists of a series of marketing committees fixing quotas, prices, subsidies, all on classic Fascist lines and openly declared to be such by Mr. Elliott himself.

The latest measure, of course, is the Unemployment Insurance Act of 1934. The most outstanding feature of the Act is its

essentially Fascist character, not merely in that
it has slashed the unemployed workers, and
developed the abominable family " Means
Test " principle, but by the establishment of
the Unemployment Assistance Board it has
struck a most powerful blow at the democratic
rights of the people. The Board is appointed
and not elected. Parliament has no control
over it and its administration. Members of
Parliament can no longer raise questions concerning its administration on behalf of their
constituents. Nor can the local councils or
councillors do anything in the matter. Public
assistance now relates to all those who were on
transitional benefit on 1st January, 1935, and
who may claim it afterwards, and a large number
of those previously under the Public Assistance
Committee now come under the Unemployment Assistance Board. Courts of Referees
and Appeal are not elected, but selected. The
whole question of unemployment relief, therefore, comes under a dictatorship, and democracy
on this question is frustrated. The workers are
thus driven into mass protests as the only
means of challenge to its administration, only
to find that in anticipation the powers of
suppression have been made more Fascist in

character, the police having been made into a ruling class force with carefully selected officers trained in loyalty to their class.

In the light of these developments the tendencies in the Trade Unions assume a tremendous importance.

Between 1918 and 1927 the voice of those who advanced the theory of increasing democratization of the State was very faint. The polarity of the classes and the nakedness of the State dictatorship of capital was too obvious to need emphasizing. The Trade Unions were heavily defeated. All the aspirations of the workers for the control of industry so prominent in the first period were remembered but feebly.

Then, after the collapse of the General Strike, a further swift change took place in the policy of the State, the employers, and the Trade Unions. Direct mass action in the form of strikes was reduced to a minimum. Both Government leaders and employers, who a short time earlier had threatened to " crush the unions with all the powers of the State ", and who had actually called into action army, navy, and police against them, proposed collaboration with the defeated unions. The Trade Union leaders responded in the name of " industrial peace ". It was as if the State and the employers had succeeded in knocking into the heads of the Trade Unionists that their job was to subordinate their claims to the necessity of restoring the system and to forget their flirtations with Socialism. The latter was relegated to the confines of the Labour Party and the distant future.

The most recent Congress of the Trade Unions has not revealed any change from this outlook. Mr. Conley, the President of the Trades Union Congress, said during its proceedings in 1934 :—

> " We are not concerned with chimerical notions of ushering in a social millennium, but with organizing the wage-earners and using the power of our organization to secure for them positive, practical, and immediate benefits."

There is no doubt as to where Socialism has been relegated in the minds of Mr. Conley and other leaders. It has become nothing more than an ideal without any relation to the " practical " things Trade Unions have to do to-day. It is said and truly said that a people

without vision perish. This applies to Trade
Unions also.

On the principles enunciated they proceeded
to collaborate with the State and the employers
immediately after the great defeat of 1926.
In the forefront of the new method stood the
Federation of British Industries, the Confederation of Employers' organizations, and the
Trades Union Congress. The first result of the
new *rapprochement* was known as the Mond-
Turner agreement.   The essence of this
agreement consists of setting out ways and
means for the collaboration of employers and
employed in securing the prosperity of British
capitalist industry at home and abroad—
how to improve trade, finance, taxation, co-
ordination of social resources, trade facilities,
etc. No highfalutin schemes for the gentle-
men—just " practical, positive, immediate
benefits " for the employer with hopes for the
worker.

For example, the General Council of the
Trades Union Congress along with the Federation of British Industries sent a memorandum to
the Prime Minister, giving their views as to what
policy should be adopted at the World Economic
Conference.   The principal features of the

proposals include " cancellation of Inter-
Governmental Debts ", a " regulated exchange
governed by the level of wholesale prices ",
" stabilization of price-levels *after* wholesale
prices have been raised to a ' suitable level ',"
the planning of the economic system, " satis-
factory arrangements for short and long term
credits."

Where the workers' interests came in for
consideration or what the project had to do
with the fundamental aims of the Trade Unions
as defined in the Trades Union Congress
constitution it is difficult to discover. The
Government invited the General Council to
appoint two representatives to a panel of
industrial advisers to the United Kingdom
delegation. The General Council appointed
Mr. Walkden and Mr. Citrine.

The close working of the unions with the
State in this period has strengthened the
impression in the minds of many Trade Union
leaders in particular of the possibilities of a
partnership of the Trade Unions with the
capitalist State. This idea has been rationalized
into a philosophy of functional allocation of
responsibilities within the State.

Mr. Milne-Bailey outlines it as follows :

" It is contemplated that in future there will be a great deal more emphasis than in the past upon the development of semi-autonomous functional groups within the State. It is thought that these groups, in the form of statutory associations or corporations, . . . will be responsible for the performance of functions within the field delimited for them. It is not contemplated that Parliament and the machinery of Government as a whole will be ' functionalized ' or will cease to be representative of and responsible to the people voting as citizens. It is thought, however, that Parliament, modernized in certain ways to drop obsolete and troublesome procedure without losing any of its democratic features, will be surrounded with a network of consultative and advisory bodies, able to speak with expert knowledge of specific interests and functions. In the economic field, which will be very important but not the sole field in which this principle will operate, the National Economic Council, on which Trade Unionism will be strongly represented, will act in such capacity. In matters especially effecting Trade Union interests the General Council of the Trades Union Congress itself will be recognized as the authoritative body to advise on behalf of organized Labour, as individual unions will be on questions of particular concern to Labour in specific industries. As the area of interest and expert knowledge narrows, the more the specialized institutions will be the appropriate advisory bodies.

" The Trade Union organizations, then, will be neither agents of the State nor entirely outside bodies playing a critical and hostile role. They will remain autonomous institutions, within the general framework that has been described, but with functions that link them to the State in a consultative and constructive way.

" As the planning of the economic life proceeds . . . the Trade Union movement will also assume new functions *within* industry. Each Public Corporation will secure the participation of organized Labour either by direct representation of the unions on the supreme controlling board or by some other mechanism of a similar kind, as desired by the unions concerned. In addition there will be a network of consultative bodies, works councils, and the like to which the unions will appoint members. . . .

" It will be seen that the main principle under-lying these suggestions is that where the interests of Labour are most directly and concretely affected, the unions will actively participate and that where general policies and the wider economic issues of Government are concerned, the Trade Union Movement will have a recognized consultative and advisory role. . . ." [1]

This outline of gradualism *in excelsis* proceeds upon the assumption that such a thing as economic antagonisms in capitalism are not fundamental but just irritating pin-pricks that can be made acceptable by a few cushions of consultation. There is apparently no such thing as a crisis of capitalism, but only maladjustments that can easily be remedied with the provision of more facilities for discussion. The differences between Socialism and capitalism are not fundamental but are due to the refusal on the part of irresponsible socialists and capitalists to see that Socialism and capitalism are really one and the same thing.

There is a great similarity in the scheme outlined by Mr. Bailey to that state of affairs which obtained during the War. But the outstanding difference between the position of the Trade Unions then and now lies in the fact that the State in war-time must dominate completely and the extraordinary economic

[1] *Trade Unions and the State*, pp. 378–9.

conditions and market relations are totally different from those of peace-time. The War swallowed all that was produced. The unemployed were absorbed in industry or scattered on the battlefields. To-day there is no inexhaustible market swallowing the products of industry. There exists the fiercest competition between large scale capitalist enterprises, an economic crisis, and vast unemployment ; weakened powers of resistance of the workers to economic pressure. Moreover, the Trade Unions are held in the grip of repressive legislation.

This is not the growth of political democracy and functional devolution. It constitutes the sharpening of class relations and the rapid approach of the critical hour when the Trade Unions and the whole Labour Movement have to see not only that there is a difference between Socialism and capitalism but also that they have to be prepared to use their power to achieve Socialism.

The relations of the Trade Unions to the State in the present period are thus full of contradictions. As organs of a class whose interests are opposed to those represented by the State, the Trade Unions are repeatedly thrust into conflict with it. The declared aims of Socialism coincide with that opposition and point to the need for a State power of the opposite political character to that of the present to fulfil its aims. At the same time the outlook and policy as expressed by Trade Union leaders and Congress decisions is that of attempting to rehabilitate the system to which they should be opposed and working with forces they are pledged to conquer.

And this is at a time when the outlines of the Corporate State of Fascism are becoming clearly defined in the policy of the ruling class.

Chapter V

TRADE UNIONS AND STRIKES

FROM the moment Trade Unions came into existence the strike has always been their principal weapon. The " right to strike " has always stood in the forefront of Trade Union experience and behind all negotiations, bargains, and settlements. Indeed, all Trade Union power rests upon the common will of Trade Unionists to " withdraw their labour ". It is a " right " which cannot be taken away. It can be legally fettered. Intimidation may make it difficult but the exercise of the common will to cease work, which is the essence of working class combination, is inalienable.

Other means than the strike may have been adopted by the Trade Unions to achieve their objects. Propaganda, agitation, political persuasion, all come within the category of Trade Union activities to secure their aims, but the strike weapon remains basic, though it may be used only " as a last resort ".

Before we consider the various forms of strikes and their significance, it is important to realize whence this form of action derives its importance. It is considered by some recent apologists that Trade Unions arise more from vocational economic relationships than from class relationships. What are the facts ? Class relationships are based upon property relationships, and the peculiar characteristic of all wage workers is the proletarian or propertyless feature of their economic position in society. By the very nature of their position within capitalism they must sell their labour power to the owners of the means of production, and this necessity applies to all workers irrespective of their vocation. It was precisely this fact that gave rise to Trade Unions. Had it been merely a question of the " self-expression " of the workers in their vocations then there would have been " weavers unions ", " agricultural workers unions ", and the like before the industrial revolution. It was the creation of a proletarian class, the establishment of a new property relationship, which brought the Trade Unions into existence. The vocational aspect of union organization was due to the form and incidence in which the new class relationship expressed itself and has no wider significance. It is a factor which becomes of less and less content the greater the integration of industry and the more the property relationship becomes the central question upon which all economic and political issues turn.

The struggle of the early craftsmen and tradesmen was not a struggle to make good craftsmen, it was a struggle against exploitation. The fight to limit apprentices was an economic fight against the operation of the economic law of supply and demand to the detriment of the craftsmen. It had little indeed to do with their vocational interests. Even the struggle for " good working materials " engaged in from time to time has had a deep economic basis although the workers have sincerely desired to work on good materials because undoubtedly they prize the greater æsthetic satisfaction thus afforded to them. But capitalism offers little scope for æsthetic considerations in production and the revolt against bad materials has been stirred far more by the effect on earnings than æsthetics.

With the growth of the machine industry and the increasing division of the labour process the vocational form of organization has been greatly modified and the largest of Trade Union organizations assume the industrial or general labour form. It is patent and obvious that the vast majority of the struggles of the unions are struggles for improving the price of the commodity " labour power " and all questions of vocational interest are subordinate to this issue. This applies as much to the modern unions as to the early struggles. True, the average worker wants to like his vocation, but ninety-nine times out of a hundred he curses it, because of the incessant vitiation of his interest by the competitive relations of capitalism. On the vocational interests of the worker it will be necessary to dwell in a further chapter on " Workers' Control of Industry ", suffice it at this stage to emphasize that the basis of the Trade Union struggles is the *class* basis. The form of the Trade Unions may be largely vocational, but their struggles transcend the vocational structure and epitomize class issues and they must do so until the property issue is solved by social ownership. Then, with the cessation of the exploitation of man by man, can and will vocational interests find free and full expression.

In assessing the significance of strikes, it is important to realize that they have been varied

in form, character, and extent. There have
been short strikes and strikes of long duration.
There have been those which have been confined
to the members of a local craft union. There
have been countless strikes of national Trade
Unions, sympathetic strikes, political strikes,
general strikes. But all of them have meant
the withholding of the commodity " labour
power " from the service of the owners of the
means of production : they have all been forms
of the class struggle.

Strikes will vary in their importance according
to their dimensions, the circumstances under
which they are waged, their duration, and the
extent to which they strengthen the workers
in the fight against the employers. Although
in the early years of the history of Trade Unions
strikers were severely punished, the later history
reveals an indifference on the part of employers
and the State to small-scale strikes, but the
political strike and the general strike have
roused deep hostility in the ranks of the ruling
class. And the reason is clear.

There are those who define the character
of a strike by the declared aim of the strikers.
This method had led to much controversy in
Labour ranks especially after the General Strike

of 1926. This strike was a sympathetic strike in support of the miners who refused wage reductions. The General Council of the Trades Union Congress insisted that the General Strike was purely an " industrial strike ". That it was a strike of industrial workers is true. That its declared aims were industrial is beyond dispute. But we cannot judge the full significance of a strike by what the strikers think of themselves or their aims. As well might we value a person by what he thinks of himself, as measure the significance of a strike on such a principle. A general strike cannot be merely an industrial stoppage. When millions of workers simultaneously cease work at the bidding of an authority other than the State it means a challenge to the authority of the State. No Government can stand by under such circumstances and watch the machinery of production come to a standstill without taking up the challenge to its authority. It is this fact which takes the issue of the economic aim of the strike into the political field. To wage a general strike means to marshal class against class. The moment the struggle has passed into a trial of strength it must become a challenge to the political authority, namely the State.

The pioneers of the theory of the general strike had no illusions about this question. William Benbow who put it forward as a "general holiday", in what is familiarly known as the period of revolutionary Trade Unionism at the beginning of the nineteenth century, advocated it as the means of social revolution. He wrote, "There will not be insurrection ; it will simply be passive resistance. The men may remain at leisure ; there is, and can be, no law to compel them to work against their will. They may walk the streets or fields with their arms folded, they will wear no swords, carry no muskets ; they will present no multitude for the Riot Act to disperse. They merely abstain, when their funds are sufficient, from going to work for one week or one month ; and what happens in consequence ? Bills are dishonoured, the *Gazette* teams with bankruptcies, capital is destroyed, the revenue fails, the system of Government falls into confusion, and every link in the chain which binds society together is broken in a moment by this inert conspiracy of the poor against the rich." The general strike was thus conceived as a means of effecting a social revolution and bringing about the greatest conceivable political, economic, and social changes.

Whether of itself the general strike can do that is another matter. It must be fairly clear to the reader that such a negative form of action could not possibly succeed in its objective of the transformation of society for a variety of reasons. It assumes that the Government with all the forces of the State at its disposal would adopt a passive attitude. But in such circumstances the Government must act at once and would act at once, as a matter of self-preservation. It would seek alternative forces for the manning of various industries for the supply of the means of life. It would call on the army, navy, and police and voluntary supplementary forces to run skeleton services. It would mobilize the press and all organs of publicity. It would prohibit the workers from issuing papers, arrest their leaders under the various conspiracy acts, intimidate the strikers, etc.

The idea of carrying through a social revolution by means of a folded arms policy is romantic. When the idea was first advanced it was certainly a striking advance on the little sectional strikes which had marked the history of Trade Unionism up to that time. The vision of the new order was a big advance from that of the machine breakers and the small bargaining policy of the early Trade Unionists.

Benbow and his colleagues did not realize that to carry through a social revolution by means of the General Strike it was necessary not only to have a political programme but the conditions which would make such a programme possible of realization. A revolution without an all national crisis in which the armed forces of the State have become " disaffected " and the capitalists can no longer govern as before, and without a working class politically conscious and willing to " face the last fight " without a general staff, i.e. a party supported by the mass organizations of the workers prepared for the most drastic forms of action, cannot hope to beat the forces of the old State and create the new State power. A general strike has either to be a demonstration of short duration or the first steps towards the taking of power by the working class. It may be the means of exerting mass pressure on the Government of the day but such mass pressure would have to be strictly limited or pass into the more serious stage of the direct struggle for power. To enter on the preparations for a general strike without a due recognition of these facts is to pave the way to defeat.

The history of strikes fully bears out this analysis and these conclusions. In the early stages of British Trade Union history when Benbow propagated the " general holiday " this method failed precisely for the above reasons. There was no party of the workers equipped in theory and practice with the art of revolution, to function as the general staff of the army of the working class. The mass strikes were an accumulation of local strikes on distinctive economic issues. It was too early in the history of the workers' movement for the creation of a party to lead the class.

The strikes of the nineteenth century were, in the main, Trade Union strikes for the sectional interests of the workers. They were fought out by a trial of strength between the employers and the workers, the State cracking the whip of the law and occasionally giving them a severe cut, as, for example, with the Criminal Law Amendment Act. After the passing of the 1871 law legalizing strike action, it proceeded to punish the strikers with the new law for attempting to make the strikes effective.

General strikes do not make their appearance until the beginning of the twentieth century, although there was a general strike in Belgium in 1893. The aim of this strike was to bring pressure on the Government to secure universal suffrage, and was partly successful. There were general strikes in Sweden and Holland in 1902 and 1903 which were limited to demonstrative action of agreed duration. The Swedish strike of 1902 is of special interest because it was called at the behest of the Socialist Party of Sweden on a political issue before the Swedish Parliament.

The general strike in Holland in 1903 was defeated because of bad organization. But it is of importance because of the issue involved. The Government was projecting legislation to prevent strikes in the public services. The Trade Unions took exception to this and were defeated. This action of the Holland Government was a precursor of what was to follow very quickly in other countries.

The growth of industry was massing the workers together in ever-larger numbers. The greater the growth of industry the greater also the growth of " public services " controlled by the State. The " public services " were staffed by wage labour and the workers in them were subject to the operation of the same economic laws as the rest of the working class, although a number of concessions were given to them for political reasons, the principal one of which was a certain regularity of employment. They accordingly also organized themselves in Trade Unions and became part of the organized working class movement.

This alarmed the ruling class since it would impede the centralized control of the State machine in the event of any big dispute with the working class. To have the Civil Service in alliance with the industrial masses they conceived to be almost as dangerous to the authority of the State as the alliance of the army and navy with the workers, especially in this period when disputes achieved such dimensions that almost every conflict rapidly passed from a dispute between the workers and the employers into a dispute with the State.

A comparison of the pre-War strikes with those of post-War years reveals a most remarkable constrast. Before the War the State was rarely called upon to interfere. It could afford to remain unconcerned in the disputes which followed the collapse of the Chartist Movement

in the 'forties right up to the War. After the
War the situation had changed. The first big
clash was the Forty-hour Strike. This rapidly
developed into a Scottish general strike and
saw the State interfere on a large scale. Glasgow
was transformed into a military camp. After
about ten days the strike was defeated though
its moral effect on the rest of the working class
movement was enormous. In 1919 the great
railway strike took place. This was a direct
conflict with the State for the railways were
still under government control. It ended in
a compromise. The miners' strike of 1921 was
directed against the mine owners and the State
and against the de-control of the mines by the
State. Here again the issue was not pushed to
a conclusion. State interference and control
of the issues involved occurred in the disputes
in the cotton and woollen industries in 1929,
whilst the General Strike of 1926 followed by
the seven months' continuation of the miner's
lock-out stand out as of enormous significance
in the class battles of post-War years.

The General Strike of 1926 was the greatest
act of workers' solidarity known in the history
of this country. It arose out of a dispute
concerning the wages of the miners. From the

first the State was brought into action, and
appeared as the open ally of the mine owners.
The miners were taking a stand against wage
reductions and the lengthening of the working
day. The whole Trade Union Movement stood
firmly behind them. The State prepared for
a first class struggle. Finding itself unready for
decisive action in 1925 it advanced a subsidy of
£25,000,000 to cover the cost of maintaining the
status quo for nine months pending preparation.
The conflict was precipitated in the spring of
1926. The Strike began on 1st May. It lasted
nine days. Army, Navy, Emergency Powers,
the Organization for the Maintenance of Supplies
for strike breaking were all brought into
action. The country was very close to a civil
upheaval.

The workers were beaten. The miners stood
firm for seven months more but in the end they
also were defeated. The Government immediately decided to follow up the advantages
gained after the collapse of the General Strike.
The workers were unable to strike back. It
passed the 1927 legislation which tore the Trade
Unions in the Civil Service out of the control
of the Trades Union Congress and the Labour
Party, forbade political strikes, made sympathetic

action illegal, controlled picketing, and created new crimes.

It appears to me, therefore, to be an obvious conclusion to draw from these events the lesson that the greater the development of industry and the closer the massing of the workers in the towns, the greater is the prospect of mass conflict with the State, and the more society reveals the appearance of two forces mobilized against each other. The State stands at the head of one force representative of property-holders, the leaders of labour at the head of the workers' army massed in the Trade Unions.

It must also be clear that the more this process continues the more politically significant do the strikes become. The keen anxiety of the capitalists to devise means of collaboration with the workers' organizations to-day should therefore be regarded not as due to a change of heart but as a symptom of their fear of the logical development of the strike. Despite all the fluctuations of the strike waves throughout the history of capitalism the main curve of their development is in the direction of larger and larger general strikes. The nearer the approach to a revolutionary crisis the more likely is this to characterize labour struggles.

This, of course, is the logic of the development of a system based on economic contradictions. Large-scale industry masses the exploited workers together in ever-larger numbers. Their organizations consequently cover a larger body of workers and once set in motion draws into action still larger numbers of workers. The more acute the class relations which arise from the economic crisis the greater is the likelihood of still larger scale conflicts possessing all the potentialities of a revolutionary upheaval.

Other features of the history of strikes are of considerable importance in considering the relation of strikes to revolutionary upheavals. So long as the strikes were confined to small sections of workers there was nothing of outstanding importance in the form and activity of the strike committees in the localities where the strikes were conducted. But the post-War strikes, because of their dimensions and the effect of their class solidarity and appeal to the workers, developed new organs of control which can only be described as embryonic " workers councils ". So complete was the " Forty-hour Strike " of 1919 in Belfast that the whole city for several days passed almost entirely into the hands of the strike committees which enlarged their functions and took upon themselves the responsibility for the maintenance of order, lighting of the city, and the feeding of the people.

Again in the movement of the masses which threatened a political general strike to stop the war on Soviet Russia in 1920, there were established up and down the country what were known as " councils of action " which represented a coming together of all the workers' political and industrial organizations ready for the general strike. In form and character they were a close approximation to the " Soviet ". This " soviet " form of organization which develops with the General Strike was still more clearly outlined in the great strike of the German workers in 1920 against the Kapp–Lutwich " putsch ".

The period of the small strikes in the middle of the nineteenth century gave rise to the Trades Councils ; the mass strikes of the twentieth century are giving rise to the councils of action. The development along these lines follows necessarily the course of the mass-actions of the workers and the changed relationship to the State. It is not in contradiction to the development of their political activities for the conquest of government by Parliamentary action but supplementary or, shall I say, parallel to it.

There is, indeed, an intimate connection between the two forms of advance being made by the Labour Movement. They are not separate from each other as many people would like to have us believe. Nor are they alternative forms of action. They are both reflexes of the one struggle against exploitation, the character of which varies according to circumstance. From the moment that the political consciousness of the working class crystallized into the formation of its own political party every great period of strike action has had its sequel in sweeping advances in the political arena. The political advancement of Labour has had its own reaction on the strikes and intensified the political significance of the strikes in the minds of the workers. The strikes and political action act and react upon each other, and the outcome, in relation both to the conquest of power by the workers and to the forms of government which will ensue, may be totally different from the generally accepted belief in the Labour Movement itself. But that opens up questions to be dealt with in a later chapter.

CHAPTER VI

TRADE UNIONS AND POLITICS

ONE of the most remarkable transformations of a political situation in any country was the sudden and complete collapse of political activity in the British working class after 1842. There had been more than twenty years of tremendous mass activity. No one can deny either the extent or the intensity of the political struggle of that period. The agitation for the Reform Bill of 1832 and the Charter, both of which were great programmes of political reforms, embraced millions of people. Every form of mass action had been brought into play—strikes, demonstrations, petitions, and violence. Then suddenly all was quiet.

The economic basis for the changed attitude is easily discernible as one looks back on the history of the period, but even when that is recognized the extent of the slump in political interest was remarkable. At the same time it is worth while to note the contents of the political programme of the Chartists. The Charter itself was extracted from the programme of the "National Union of the Working Class", which later became better known as the London Working Men's Association. Its programme consisted of the following :—

"(1) To avail itself of every opportunity in the progress of society, for the securing for every working man the full value of his labour and the disposal of the produce of his labour.

"(2) To protect working men against the tyranny of the master and manufacturers by all just means as circumstance may determine.

"(3) To obtain for the nation an effectual reform in the House of Commons of the British Parliament, Annual Parliament, extension of the suffrage to every adult male, vote by ballot, and especially no property qualification for members of Parliament.

"(4) To propose petitions, addresses, and demonstration to the Crown and both Houses of Parliament."

This was, despite the phrases of the first demand, essentially a democratic reform policy which cannot be described in any way as

extravagant.   The violent reaction to politics
could arise only as a revolt against the methods
of the leaders for the attainment of the
objectives.

The leaders were divided in policy between
moral persuasion and the use of physical force.
The great conventions of the Chartists were
thus always face to face with the issue of what
was to be the next step after the demonstrations
and the presenting of petitions.   There was no
outlet for them in the Parliamentary institution
for it was for this outlet and means of developing their movement that they aspired.   The
physical force group felt they could advance
only through civil war but were not equipped
for so great a venture.   The moral force group
had nothing to offer beyond propaganda of the
word and shrank from the logic of the physical
force proposals.

Hence after repeated demonstrations which
ended only in words and the crushing of the
physical force Chartists by the Government
forces, the reaction of the masses to the helpless-
ness of their leaders was most profound.   It was
this which led to their concentration on economic
questions such as wages, hours of labour, etc.,
and the spread of Trade Unionism of a most

narrow type. The change of the general economic situation into a period of rapid trade expansion facilitated this development. The new type of leader appeared who stood for the Liberal " square deal " on the " bread and butter question " and left " politics to the politicians ".

How the Trade Union struggles against the various Trade Union Acts helped to drive the unions into political action and the formation of the Labour Party has already been dealt with, but it is necessary to remember that this struggle was not conducted under the banner of Socialism. Socialist opinion and propaganda were confined to a very small minority of the workers. A few of the old Chartists such as Jones and Harvey continued to carry the Red Flag in the ranks of the Fraternal Democrats and the First Workers' International. The propaganda for a working class party was developed considerably by the First International, but the theoretical views of the Trade Union leaders who first supported the proposal for independent Labour representation were really the views of Liberals. Groups of socialists tried to build socialist parties, but with little success. The Fabian Society, with Sidney Webb and G. B. Shaw at the head, the Social

Democratic Federation, led by H. M. Hyndman, the Independent Labour Party, led by Keir Hardie, all carried onward a great deal of socialist propaganda and worked incessantly for a Labour Party. Within their ranks a variety of theories concerning State Socialism, reform, and revolution, ways and means, etc., were held. They prepared the ground for the Trade Union acceptance of political action, but it was not until the beginning of the twentieth century that the real mass break with the old order began.

It began with the formation of Labour Representation Committees. After the victories of 1906, the Labour Party, in name and fact, began its career, but it was a party without a programme until 1918. Outlined by S. Webb in *Labour and the New Social Order*, the first programme was drafted with an eye on the Trade Unions. It emphasized such reforms as " the universal application of the National Minimum Wage ", the universal application of a prescribed minimum of health, leisure, education, and subsistence, Factory Acts, Health Acts, Education Acts, etc., etc., only tentatively and gradually did it venture to advance the nationalization of industries and then only of those " which had reached the most advanced stage of monopoly and concentration ".

In this programme there was no recognition of any crisis of capitalism. Starting from the " bread and butter " point of view ascribed to Trade Unionists, it proceeded with a graduation of change of such slowness and sureness that the new system must dawn without anybody knowing it had arrived after generations of prosperous capitalism. It was Owen's " thief in the night " disguised as a gentle ghost pervading the house.

The programme did give a little scope to the demands for the " democratic control of industry " because the Trade Unions were growing rapidly and were demanding a place in the factories, mills, and mines as well as Parliament. The democratic control of industry envisaged was, however, to be a kind of appendage to the Parliamentary system, an increasing representation of the Trade Unions in State departments of nationalized industries with not so much emphasis placed on the part to be played by the " man on the job ".

There has always been a certain theoretical conflict between the convinced socialists and the Trade Unionists and a contradiction between the deeds of the Labour Movement and the words of the theoreticians of both schools of thought. The Trade Unions generally have stood firmly for the policy of securing immediate economic gains and the defence of standards already won, and one must consider closely where this has led and whither it is leading.

Let our considerations start from the truism that the success of such a policy depends upon a progressively developing economic system. To be pressing continually for economic advantage for the workers from a system in decline must lead to terrific class conflicts and threaten the existence of the system itself.

It may be argued that the system is not in decline and that the assumption which runs through this book is entirely wrong. This is not an economic treatise and I do not propose to attempt an exhaustive analysis in order to prove this assumption. Nevertheless, it may be worth while to advance here a few important considerations and facts to substantiate this view.

The principal economic factor establishing a condition of crisis is the increasing dispro-portion between production and the market capacity of the system, a state of affairs arising from the private property relations which govern capitalist society. Although the rate of production per head has increased enormously and tends to increase still more rapidly under modern methods of industrial rationalization and mechanization, the market continues to contract. So much is this the case that crops both of raw materials and consumption goods and quantities of the means of production are deliberately destroyed with a view to raising prices for the restricted production.

In the cotton, woollen, and shipbuilding industries of this country, companies have been formed to destroy plant and machinery and the destruction of crops from land and sea is common. The facts and the policy are not hidden. Mr. Neville Chamberlain explained the situation most cryptically in a speech in the House of Commons on 2nd June, 1933, when he said :

" To allow production to go on unchecked and unregulated when it could almost at a moment's notice be increased to an almost indefinite extent was absolutely folly."

A most consoling explanation to the unemployed millions ! At the same time the increased rate of production reduces the number of workers necessary for production. Hence the accentuation of the growth of a permanent vast army of unemployed workers in all capitalist countries.

These contradictions are further aggravated by the fact that the international market has exhausted its capacity for expansion owing to the inner development of the various countries of the world which to-day produce goods previously imported. This has led to the growth of economic nationalism behind the frontiers of which each country seeks to be self-contained on the basis which demands international expansion. Each country desires increased exports, but, driven into economic nationalism against imports in favour of " home production ", that which it desires in the form of exports it must perforce deny itself. Hence the stupidities of high tariffs, quota systems, prohibitions, currency manipulations, etc., and the intensification of the competition for the restricted market.

The dilemma of the capitalist world was expressed by Sir Alfred Ewing in his Presidental Address to the British Association in 1932. He said, " And the world finds itself glutted with competitive commodities produced in a quantity too great to be absorbed. Where shall we look for a remedy ? I cannot tell."

The problem can be illustrated in another way. The average production per man of pig iron in this country in 1920 was nearly two hundred tons, and of steel castings 54 tons. Seven years later the average had risen to three hundred tons of pig iron per man and 86 tons of steel.

In 1924 the miner produced 17·59 cwt. of coal per shift for 10s. 7d. In 1933 he produced 22·45 cwt. of coal per shift for 9s. 1½d.

In July, 1934, not less than 519 persons per 10,000 of the population were in receipt of Poor Law Relief as compared with 190 per 10,000 in 1913.

Meanwhile the *Economist* reports that 257 companies during May, 1934, showed a percentage increase of profits over the previous year of 23·43 per cent.

These figures of contrast are not peculiar to Britain. They are typical of capitalist countries in general. The net result is to increase all the international antagonisms both economic and political. The more economic nationalism, which finds its sharpest form in Fascism, grows the more tense must become the international political situation. The growing demand for a redistribution of territory between the powers is the natural reflex of the limitations set by the Versailles Treaty accelerated by economic nationalism.

Thus the pace is set towards the stimulation of war industries which is a big factor in producing responsibility for the trade " boomlet " of to-day, the piling up of armaments (witness the rise in share values of all aircraft and armament firms and chemical manufacturers and the increased budget expenditure on " defence "), and the war which is not far ahead.

Nor is the capitalist world's chaos limited by these developments towards war. Internally each country under the strain of these economic and political contrasts and tensions is marked by the fear of the ruling class of social upheavals and revolution.

This is the basis for the animosity of the ruling classes towards the Soviet Union which, having solved its economic problems on socialist lines and prevented the transformation of Russia into a colony of the powers, profoundly influences the masses of the world suffering from the chaos of capitalism in the direction of Socialism.

These facts alone, in the writers opinion, establish the contention that we live in a declining system and are heading towards a decisive stage of crisis upon which depends the fate of generations of our kind.

A study of the Trades Union Congress reports since the War reveals the contradiction between the logic of circumstance and opinion and policy. The whole Labour Movement (Party, Trade Union, and Co-operatives) has based its political policy upon the fundamentally false premise of a capitalist recovery and the probable prosperous development of capitalism into Socialism. This view has been challenged repeatedly in many conferences and congresses but it has always remained the basis of policy.

It is impossible, however, for a class movement such as the Trade Union Movement to live with its head in the clouds perpetually echoing capitalist opinion, hopes, and fears. It has time and again been compelled to act contrary to its theory and to follow the logic of the class relations rising from the development of the crisis of the system. For example, the competitive relations of capitalism have repeatedly demanded wage reductions and the lengthening of the working hours. The Trade

Unions have resisted in most peculiar circumstances despite the theories held by them. In 1926 they gave the greatest shock it has ever had to the stability of the whole system of capitalism in this country by declaring the General Strike and yet nothing could have been more contradictory to the policy held in reality at the time and declared by the secretary of the Trade Union Congress at the Brighton Congress in 1933 when he said :

" It was very simple to talk about organizing strikes to obtain wage increases in an industry that until recently was able statistically to prove that there were not profits available to give wage increases."

Here was the whole case for the mine owners in 1926.

Still more contradictory, if that were possible, was the situation between 1929 and 1931. The Labour Government was the product of the victories of a party which rested upon the Trade Unions. Prominent Trade Unionists, such as Mr. J. H. Thomas, Mr. J. R. Clynes, and Miss Bondfield, were in the Government. The Parliamentary Labour Party was composed largely of Trade Union representatives. Yet the Government, pursuing a policy based upon the theory of gradual advance, a theory accepted by the unions, which leads inevitably, in the present period, to wage reduction met with the most stubborn opposition from the unions. Great disputes occurred in the woollen and cotton industries with the government willy nilly taking part in an attack upon wages which the Trade Unions actually resisted. They lost in the struggle to the extent of seven and a half per cent cut in the cotton industry and ten per cent in the woollen industry.

Finally, when the stability of the system received another blow by a sudden plunge into a deeper phase of the economic crisis it was the Trade Unions which pulled down the Labour Government. The General Council of the Trades Union Congress rejected the proposed " economies " advanced by the deputation of the Government and its economists which were in fact the logical development of their own theories.

Such confusion and contradiction could not have happened had there been a consistent political policy based upon a correct analysis of the nature of the crisis of the system and the tendencies within it. Despite the fact that the crisis of capitalism had become more and more demonstrably incapable of solution in terms of capitalism, the Labour Movement proceeded as if there were no crisis and the possibilities of recovery and the gradual modification of capitalism into Socialism remained a tenable policy.

It is a strange thing, one of the most remarkable examples of political myopia in history, that a mighty movement such as the British Labour Movement should be gathering its millions of supporters with increasing momentum as a result of a crisis it refuses to recognize as a crisis of the system. After a short spell of revolutionary temper in the Labour Party following the collapse of the Labour Government in 1931 and an exhibition of satisfaction on the part of the General Council of the Trades Union Congress that it had stood against the Government " economy cuts ", the Party and the Union have resumed the " gradualist " policy, but not without giving another example of contradiction and confusion which it would be hard to excel.

The Trades Union Congress at Brighton in September of 1933, passed the following resolution :—

" This Congress records its strongest protests against the continued failure of the present Government to take effective measures against unemployment, to support the proposal for the forty-hour week and the construction of useful public works, and to produce a positive policy for promoting the recovery of industry and trade.

" Whilst reaffirming our belief that social ownership and control furnishes the only adequate and lasting solutions to the problems Congress appreciates the significance of the vigorous efforts now being made by President Roosevelt towards the stimulation and regulation of industry by means of the Industrial Recovery Act and allied legislation ; it welcomes the recognition given in that legislation and in the ' codes of practice ' promulgated thereunder, to the Trade Union policy of reducing working hours as a means of diminishing unemployment, and of raising wages as a means of increasing purchasing power.

" Congress congratulates the American Trade Unions upon their energetic assertion of the workers' rights to bargain collectively through their own independent organization.

Congress expresses the hope that with the co-operation of the Trade Unions, President Roosevelt will be able to overcome the difficulties involved in this decisive departure from the traditional individualism of American industry.

" Congress further trusts that the present British Government will pursue a similar policy by taking immediate steps to initiate useful schemes of public works financed by the use of the national credit, to enact a maximum working week of forty hours without reduction of wages : to prohibit child labour under 16 years of age, and to raise the school leaving age to 16.

" Further that the Government will set an example to employers by raising wages in the public services beginning with the restoration of the ' Economy ' cuts in wages, salaries, and social service ; to make more liberal provisions for pensioning aged workers : and generally to take all possible measures for increasing the purchasing power of the masses and for planning the economic life of the nation in the interests of the whole people."

If there is any doubt about the relationship of this policy to the outlook of the leaders of the Trades Union Congress then Mr. Citrine made it abundantly clear in introducing the resolution. He said :

> " The policy of the Congress for a period of years, modest as their contribution necessarily had to be, was towards stimulating trade recovery in the interests of their members and not in the interests of the capitalists."

The capitalists do not object and cannot object to the motive so long as there is co-operation with them to achieve the results they want. They have consistently argued that concessions to the workers depend upon the " prosperity of industry ". Mr. Citrine continued :

> " They did not believe that the policy of reorganizing industry under capitalism—that of stimulating markets and coming to agreements with international competitors—could be a lasting and complete solution of the difficulties, but it was a contribution which would be welcomed by the millions of unemployed in this country. If they could get back to 1928, while they would not have removed

the basic causes of the trouble they would earn the heartfelt gratitude of hundreds of thousands of their people.

" . . . In this resolution they called upon the British Government to take immediate action. They did not say that the British Government should follow identically what had been done in the United States. They believed that if this problem were to be attacked it ought to be attacked not by a wave of emotionalism but by careful planning and thinking. They could not put the destinies of a nation right in a few months—a campaign similar to that of the United States might not if followed have the same effect. *But the direction was essentially right, and it was because direction was right* that they called upon the British Government to adopt similar measures."

In the light of the above it can hardly be regarded as an unjust statement to affirm that " back to 1928 " is not a socialist vision nor has the rest of the statement anything to do with Socialism.

The Labour Party Conference, held at Hastings a month later, rejected the conclusions

of the Trades Union Congress. Mr. Greenwood,
speaking on behalf of the Executive of the Party,
said :

" . . . the capitalist system is breaking
down under its own weight and that is not
something merely that we believe, it is something that capitalists themselves know is
happening under their eyes, and the question,
therefore, is not one as to whether you are
going to try to amend the old capitalist
system ; the real question, the real economic
question which faces the world, is whether
you are going to have a socialist system of
society, or a form of economic dictatorship
ruled by the leaders of the capitalist world
to-day, but the solution is the socialist
solution."

The delegates of the Party Conference were
preponderatingly Trade Union delegates, many
of whom had been at Brighton the month
previous. Mr. Greenwood flatly contradicted
the policy outlined by Mr. Citrine. The
confusion was complete and something had to
be done about it. Twelve months later the two
national assemblies met again.

Both reaffirmed their belief in Socialism—

afar off—and, having done that, both the Trades Union Congress and the Labour Party Conference committed themselves to a policy in keeping with the Brighton Trades Union Congress decision already quoted. The Congress of 1934 did not go back on the decisions of 1933. On the contrary it amplified them and gave more detailed attention to Public Corporations, " co-ordination " of industry, " planned capitalism," etc.

At the Southport Conference of the Labour Party, more socialist phrases were used, but one also heard the voice of trade union leaders warning those who are pursuing " chimerical " schemes that " he who pays the piper, calls the tune ".

The politics of the Trade Unions expressed in the decisions of their Congresses and of the Labour Party Conference consist of united effort with the capitalists to reorganize capitalism on the lines of public corporations, and to make the improvement of the conditions of the workers conditional on the improvement of capital. Officially speaking, the Labour Movement is marching under the banner of planned capitalism, and to the tune of high sounding socialist phrases, towards the

Corporate State, despite its proclaimed anti-Fascism.

That this is no exaggeration is not difficult to prove from leading writers and spokesmen of the Labour Party other than the Trade Union leaders already quoted. For example, Mr. Lees-Smith was a member of the Labour Cabinet in 1929–1931 and is high in the councils the Labour Party. Writing in *Current History* of of April, 1933, he says :

" The terms ' public ownership ' or ' nationalization ', it should be pointed out, have changed their meaning in England within the last few years. Until recently, nationalization has meant the control of industry by government departments working along ordinary civil service lines and subject to political influence. But Labour now believes that this is not the proper method of controlling a business undertaking, and has substituted a system of control by public corporations, a type of nationalization which meets the objections of most Liberals and many Conservatives. Under this plan an industry is controlled by a small board of carefully selected persons, who act as trustees for the nation and who conduct the day-to-day affairs of the industry with as much freedom as an ordinary board of directors. They are subject to the decisions of Parliament only when great issues of policy are raised. This combination of Socialism and business management, which all three political parties have helped to develop, has proved itself an undisputed success. The British Broadcasting Corporation, known to every householder in England as the B.B.C., is a good example of the new system.

" . . . A great change has come over British public opinion in the last five years. Belief in the competitive system has silently disintegrated everywhere and ' rationalization ' has taken its place as the creed of the leaders of industry. The late Lord Melchett (better known as Sir Alfred Mond) was more responsible than any other business leader for this change of attitude. He first set the fashion of proclaiming that the efficient and economical conduct of an industry requires that all competition within it shall be eliminated, so that it can be controlled as a whole by one central executive, with operations concentrated in the plants best adapted for the purpose. This doctrine has been accepted by moderate Conservative opinion and even by the London *Times.*

" But rationalization makes Socialism inevitable. The British public, when faced with the
choice between capitalistic monoply and public
ownership, will certainly prefer the latter, and
all governments will help the process forward.
England, within the next two generations, will
thus evolve into a socialistic State, by a series
of measures carried through by Conservative
as well as Labour governments, blessed by the
Bishops and ratified by the King, with little
apparent change to the outside world . . ."
The declarations of leaders have so often
been wrong that I have no hesitation in asserting
that this will meet with the fate of many of its
predecessors. The Trade Union Movement and
the Labour Party are based upon the working
class. The interests of the working class are
opposed to this evolution of the grand coalition
of Toryism, Liberalism, and Labour, outlined
by Mr. Smith. The Workers' Movement is
being mobilized by socialist appeal.

The average person believes these appeals.
He is not a theoretician and he expects Socialism
to be something different from capitalism,
which is continually bringing him up against
circumstances that strengthen his anti-capitalist
views. Hence when the masses once more

give authority to a Labour Government they will expect words to become deeds and fundamental changes to be made of a socialist (i.e. anti-capitalist) character. That is one great factor contradictory to the position taken up by the Labour Party and Trades Union Congress, the ignoring of which will lead to the break-up of the entire Labour Movement.

The policy of securing immediate concessions from the capitalists can in a short view be maintained just so long as the " boomlet " lasts. Once this is exhausted and the general crisis of capitalism plunges again into a deeper stage of crisis, 1931 must repeat itself in much sharper form. Capitalism must face the workers with new periods of " economies ", whilst their temper will rise and the demand for socialist change in the system will be made by the supporters of labour. The inescapability of crisis conditions inevitably means that once more the deeds of the Labour Movement will not correspond to the theories and policies now dominating the Trade Union and Labour Party.

CHAPTER VII

TRADE UNIONS AND
WORKERS' CONTROL OF INDUSTRY

THE question of the role of the trade unions in the control of industry, what it should be now and in the future, has been a burning question at many Trades Union Congresses. It is not a new question. Robert Owen advanced it long ago, and the Grand Consolidated Trade Union of the 'thirties was formed to achieve the transformation of capitalism into Socialism by means of productive co-operation. The early builders' unions had distinctive ideas on the question too. " Down with the middlemen and the contractors," they cried, " we, the workers, can make the contract so as to receive the full amount of pay for our work." " A spirit of combination has grown up among the working-classes " says the *Poor Man's Guardian* of 19th October, 1832, " of which there has been no example in former times. A grand national organization, which promises to embody the physical power of the country is silently, but

rapidly, progressing, and the object of this is
the sublimest that can be conceived, namely—
to establish for the productive classes a complete dominion over the fruits of their own
industry. Heretofore these classes have wasted
their strength in fruitless squabbles with their
employers or with one another. They have
never sought any grand object, nor have they
been united for those they sought, to obtain
some paltry rise or prevent some paltry reduction in wages has been the general aim of
their turnouts ; and the best results of their
combination, even when successful, were merely
to secure their members against actual want in
the day of sickness and of superannuation.

"   . . . But far different from the paltry
objects of all former combinations is that now
aimed at by the Congress of delegates. Their
report shows that an entire change in society
—a change amounting to a complete sub-
mission of the existing order of the world—is
contemplated by the working-classes. They
aspire to be at the top instead of at the bottom
of society—or rather that there should be no
bottom or top at all."

James Morrison wrote in the *Pioneer*, 31st
May, 1834, " The unions are of all the other

means the only mode by which universal suffrage can safely be obtained. Because it is obtained by practice, by serving an apprenticeship. Here they start to manage their affairs on a small scale before they get management of larger affairs. The growing power and growing intelligence of Trade Unions, when properly managed, will draw into its vortex all the commercial interests of the country and, in so doing, it will become by its own self-acquired importance a most influential, we might almost say dictatorial, part of the body politic. When this happens, we have gained all that we want ; we have gained universal suffrage, for if every member of the union be a constituent and the union itself becomes a vital member of the state, it instantly erects itself into a house of trades which must supply in place of the present House of Commons and direct the industrial affairs of the country, according to the will of the trades, which composed the association of industries. This is the ascendant scale by which we arrive at universal suffrage . . . with us, universal suffrage will begin in our lodges, extend to the general union, embrace the management of trade, and finally swallow up the political power."

There was then no doubt in the minds of pioneers of Trade Unionism of a century ago as to the future role of the unions, either with regard to industry or the State. They recognized the slave condition of the workers in capitalism and had faith in the worker's power and capacity to abolish the slavery and build a new society of free men—controlling industry in a classless society. That they were ahead of their time is not their fault. The issue was not so boldly stated again until the rise of the industrial unionists at the beginning of the twentieth century. Up to this time the various schools of Socialism were not too sure about the future of the unions. The most clear were Mr. and Mrs. Sidney and Beatrice Webb, who wrote in an appendix to the *History of Trade Unionism* (1876) what was a generally held view in the ranks of socialists of the 'eighties. In the management of industry the Trade Unions were to have no part. This was the business of the State department or the trained business man, who knew what the consumers wanted. The Trade Unions, however, were to look after the suffering of the workers. They said, " If the democratic State is to obtain its fullest and fairest development, it is essential that the actual needs and desires of the human agents concerned should be the main consideration in determining the conditions of employment. Here then we find the special function of the Trade Unions in the administration of industry. The simplest member of the working-class organization knows at any rate where the shoe pinches. . . . Trade Unionism adds to the long list of functions thus delegated to professional experts the settlement of the conditions on which the citizen will agree to co-operate in the national service."

These were the views of what were known as the State Socialists. It was written in 1897. By 1920 the same writers had modified their views considerably. After drawing attention to the views quoted above, they said :

" There is, in the first place, a genuine need for, and a real social advantage in giving recognition to, the contemporary transformation in the status of the manual working wage earners, on the one hand, and of the technicians on the other, as compared with that of the manager or ' captain of industry '. This change of status, which is, perhaps, the most important feature of the industrial history of the past quarter of a century, will be most easily accorded its legitimate recognition in those industries in which the profit-making capitalist proprietor is dispensed with in favour of public ownership, whether national, municipal or co-operative. This is, incidentally, an important reason for what is called ' nationalization '. It is a real social gain that the General Secretary of the Swiss Railwaymen's Trade Union should sit as one of the five members of the supreme governing board of the Swiss Railway Administration. We ourselves look for the admission of nominees of the manual workers, as well as technicians, upon the executive boards and committees, of complete equality with the other members, in all publicly owned industries and services ; not merely, or even mainly, for the sake of the advantages of the counsel and criticism that the new owners may bring from a new standpoint, but principally for the sake of both inspiring and satisfying the increasing sense of corporate self-consciousness and public spirit among all those employed in these enterprises."

This is a considerable advance but it noticeably retains the old conception of the State and its democratization. It still gives us a picture of middle-class bureaucrats running State departments, tempered by the presence of the Trade Union representatives, refined, as it were, in the washing. One still has to ask the question, " What of the man on the job ? "

The industrial unionists and syndicalists of the period prior to the War, and the shop stewards during the War, had given very definite answers to this question. The syndicalists, of course, advanced the idea of the workers in a particular industry owning and controlling it from top to bottom. The industrial unionists stood for the social ownership of the means of production and for all people becoming members of a working class. Industry was to be organized and controlled by the industrial unions. James Connolly put the then position as follows : " What the socialists realize is that under a socialist form of society the administration of affairs will be in the hands of representatives of the various industries of of the nation ; that the workers in the shops and factories will organize themselves into unions, each union compromising all the workers of a given industry in subordination to the needs of its allied trades and to the department of industry to which it belongs. That

representatives of the various departments of
industry will meet and form the industrial
administration or national government of the
country.''

This conception of the future of the unions is
the modern counterpart to the " House of
Trades ", of the revolutionary Trade Unionists
of the Chartist period. It was carried forward
into the shop steward movement of the War
period and was expounded in a pamphlet called
The Workers' Committee by the present writer.

The Russian Revolution caused most of
the revolutionaries to modify their views in the
light of Soviet experience, but at the time the
shop stewards advocated " control of the job "
by the workers, collective contracts instead of
individual contracts, power to remove foremen,
powers to control the distribution of work, etc.
They advanced the tactic of encroaching on
the control in the workshop exercised by the
employer as a means of creating a will to end
his economic power through ownership.

An adaptation of the industrial unionist
proposals was made by the guild socialists who
advocated the social ownership of the means
of production, the administration of certain
political affairs by a citizens' parliament and

the administration of industry by industrial unions or guilds, organized in an industrial assembly, subordinate to Parliament in regard to general policy.

These views represented the theoretical views of the most advanced elements within the field of Trade Unionism and Socialism in this country during the immediate pre-War, War, and post-War years. In modified form they appeared in Trade Union conference resolutions. For example, the Trade Union railwaymen demanded before a Royal Commission in 1924 " a due measure of control and responsibility in the safe and efficient working of the railway system ". The Miners' Federation in 1918 at their annual conference demanded " in the national interests to transfer the entire coal-mining industry from private ownership and control to state ownership, with joint control and administration by the workmen and the State ". Other unions followed the same line. Then came the slump in Trade Unionism— " workers' control " receded and collaboration took its place. But with the dawn of the possibility of a Labour Government with a majority and a change in the form of industry, it reappeared once again and it was discussed at

Trade Union conferences and at the Trades Union Congress. In 1931 the Transport and General Workers' Union moved the following resolution at the Trades Union Congress :

" That this Congress calls upon the Government when introducing legislation providing for the transfer of any industry or service from private ownership to common ownership and for public control, to make provision ensuring that the workers, through their Trade Union representatives, shall have an adequate and direct share in the control and administration of such industry or service."

At the Brighton Congress of the Trades Union Congress in 1933 there was a further debate on this question and the General Council in a report declared :

" (1) That as regards labour questions, including recruitments, dismissals, discipline, working conditions, etc., the Trade Unions should assume more responsibility in this sphere.

" (2) As regards technicians, commercial and financial matters, ultimate responsibilities should be in the hands of managers who satisfied proper standards including fitness to work successfully with large bodies of workers, and appointed solely because of the competence to fill the position.

" (3) That works councils be established for regular consultation on all internal matters not coming within the scope of the ordinary negotiating machinery."

The General Workers' Union, led by Mr. Dukes, carried the matter a stage farther with a demand that " Congress claims, as a statutory right, that fifty per cent of the representation on magagerial committees shall be accorded to workers' nominees, and asserts the right of the Trade Unions to retain their present powers and functions relating to conditions of employment and pay ".

Here occurred an interesting interlude. Suddenly the socialist consciousness appeared to waken in the General Council and they wanted to know whether the new proposal related to socialized industries or privately owned industries. It was recognized at once that unless socialized industries were intended, the new proposal would mean nothing other than a rehash of the Whitley proposals.

At the Hastings Conference the amendment was redrafted in order to make it clear that the proposal related to the socialized industries only. It was then passed by the Congress and has become a declared aim of the Trade Unions and the Labour Party.

These resolutions are a decided advance on previous Congress and Party decisions. They represent the reaction of Trade Unionists to the attempt to twist Socialism from its real meaning to the " modern version " of government by public corporations. They were anxious to know where the " workers came in " in the proposed new schemes. This is the essence of the fight for " workers' control ", which has taken place in the Trades Union Congress and Labour Party Conferences.

The form in which the issue has been clothed, however, is different from the content, in that the picture presented by the resolutions is that of the workers changing " bosses " and not that of a classless working community. There is a " sharing of responsibility " with some force over the workers which takes the form of a fifty-fifty arrangement of seats on the directorship and managerial committees of the corporations between the corporations and the Trade Unions' nominees.

Although the passing of this resolution was a definite set-back and challenge to those who had held the views represented by Mr. Morrison and Mr. Lees-Smith, much remains to be done before the full implications of the demand for " workers' control " is made clear in the Labour Movement.

At the same time the aim of the Trade Unions and the Labour Movement must be distinguished from policy. The aim of the whole movement is Socialism. The resolution on " workers' control of industry " has entered into the aims but the daily conduct and practice of the unions are based on other considerations.

There are now, therefore, four principal lines of thought in the working-class movement on this question of " worker's control of industry ". The main trend of the Labour Movement stands for the democratization of the capitalist state with the unions taking a greater share of responsibility for the running of industry by means of representation on its governing bodies and effecting a greater check than hitherto on conditions of labour. There is thus to be no sharp break with existing position. In short, the Trade Unions are to play a conciliatory role with regard to administration, whilst increasing responsibilities are to be undertaken in relation to modifying conditions of labour.

The logic of this view in relation to Trade Union and Labour policy, in a period when the capitalist State is shown to be rapidly evolving towards the Corporate State of Fascism, is that of rendering positive assistance to this evolution.

The second line of thought is that of the guild socialists who stand for a break with the existing order, by separating politics from industry and giving to the Trade Unions, re-organized as Industrial Unions or Guilds co-ordinated in a House of Industry or Parliament of Industry, the full responsibility for the administration of industry on a socialist basis. By these changes the workers are to be given an entirely new status, namely that of co-operators in a self-governing industry. The principle of organization according to the functions to be performed, is to govern all departments of social, industrial, and political activity.

The third view is that of the revolutionary Trade Unionists, who come nearer to the views expounded by Connolly. These hold the view that the " control of industry " turns upon the question of ownership. Unless there is social ownership there can be no " workers' control " of industry or of any other department of social activity. The question of ownership will be solved by revolutionary means, which will do away with Parliament and establish a soviet or workers' council form of government based upon an industrial or " work " franchise. The Trade Unions will in this process be transformed into industrial unions. The factory will be the unit of the unions. The factory will be the unit also of the workers' council, though the latter draws in other representatives and delegates from the various departments of social activity. Whilst the council is a wider institution embracing all who work and has a political authority not possessed by the labour unions, there is such a similarity in structure and interlocking of activity and responsibility in administration that the role of the unions corresponds neither to that visualized by the industrial unionist or the guild socialists.

In the first place the industrial unionist had no conception of the soviet or workers' council kind of State. They visualized an industrialized society administered by a parliament or congress of industrial unions. On the other hand the Guild State with its Consumers'

Parliament and Industrial Parliament encouraged a form of dual state, but both adhered to the functional principle in the structure of the State and the relationship of all institutions.

In both cases there are close similarities as well as sharp differences, due largely to the differences of outlook as to how the change from one social system to the other would come about. The industrial unionist conceived the change coming through the continuous growth of industrial unionism until, with the great majority of the working class organized " at the point of production ", i.e. in factory, mill and mine, dockland and railway depots, etc., they could at some decisive moment assume control of industry and do away with the " political State ".

The guild socialists held the view that the change can come through a socialist majority in Parliament making the bold division of labour and relegating the whole administration of economic affairs and industry to duly trans-formed unions that have become industrial unions or guilds.

The communist dismisses both these theories and affirms that the change over from one system to the other will come through civil war—the dictatorship of the capitalist and the institutions through which it finds expression will be overcome by the dictatorship of the proletariat expressed through the democratic soviets or workers' councils. Whilst the communists propagate the transformation of the Trade Unions into industrial unions and hold the view that the economic struggle of the Trade Unions in the present system merges into the general political struggle, culminating in civil war, they maintain that the unions will not be so transformed before the social revolution. Hence in the present period they can only be a contributory factor, a powerful means of developing direct mass action in the form of strikes, demonstrations, etc., from which when the revolutionary situation arrives the workers' councils—the new political authority—will arise.

There is the fourth view which visualizes the socialist conquest of political power through a parliamentary labour majority, and the use of that power to establish the social ownership of the means of production and " workers' control of industry ". The Trade Unions are to be transformed into industrial unions and become instruments of industrial administration. This

L

view I propose to develop in succeeding chapters.

All these views, of course, contrast with those held by capitalist parties and groups, whether Liberal, Tory, or Fascist. The Liberal and the Tory, standing for the preservation of the existing system, however it be modified in form, at no point go beyond consultation with the Trade Unions in terms of the master and his servants. The Whitley Council system constitutes the most radical of the schemes to which these custodians of the old world have advanced. But as this system rules out the whole question of the control of industry by the workers, there is little point in dwelling on their views.

The Fascist point of view on the Trade Unions has been so amply demonstrated in the history of Germany and Italy that it is easy to find a starting point in any study of their views. First the existing Trade Unions are not to be transformed into industrial unions in order to assume larger functions. Fascism come to power destroys the Trade Unions. With the ground cleared it is then proposed to work the functional principle on the basis of the preservation of private property and production for profit. This is to be done by the creation of industrial corporations composed of state, employers', and workers' representatives. The function of the workers' representatives is to be that of expressing grievances concerning conditions of employment and co-operating to the maximum in making the industry profitable —the function of a helot with a squeal.

Chapter VIII

THE FUTURE OF THE TRADE UNIONS IN RELATION TO THE STATE

FROM the foregoing brief analysis of outstanding features in the nature and history of the Trade Unions two questions stand out demanding answers. The first, what is to be the future relation of the Trade Unions to the State ? ; the second, what is to be the future role of the Trade Unions in relation to industry ?

I propose to discuss the first question in this chapter, and the answer must, of course, be a qualified one. It depends upon the kind of State. In Britain we have what is known as the Democratic State. The history of the relations of the Trade Unions to the State in Britain reveals at one stage a struggle to supersede it with a form of proletarian State—the " House of Trade " of the revolutionaries of the 'forties. In another lengthy period, as from 1850 to 1900, the question was hardly raised except theoretically in socialist circles. In the third period, since marked by the development of the crisis of capitalism, there have been short alternating periods of collaboration and direct conflicts between the unions and the State with a continuous growth of political effort to change the composition of the Parliamentary government.

The periods of direct mass conflict produced new developments in workers' organizations not seen hitherto. At the base of these developments were the Trade Unions. The War-time struggles produced the factory committees movement ; the political challenge of the Labour Movement to the Government in 1920 on the question of war in Russia produced the " councils of action " ; the General Strike of 1926 produced in many areas councils based on the Trades Councils which could be designated workers' councils and which were armed with authority larger than that of strike committees though rising out of them.

Were these new phenomena soviets in embryo ? Were they pointers to the way in which new organs of political authority arise out of direct class conflict ? If that be so then the student of Trade Unionism will have to examine the question of the relation of the Trade Unions to the State in a new way, and it may be that the Trade Unions, as organizations arising from the class struggle and inseparable from it, will prove to be the begetters of a new form of workers' State out of the conflict with the capitalist State. This will depend, however, entirely upon the form of the struggle between the classes and the way it is consummated in this country.

Since the General Strike of 1926 there is no doubt whatever about the trend of opinion in the working-class as to how they propose to make the change from the present system to Socialism. Despite all efforts of the Communist Party, and the Independent Labour Party, to split the Labour Movement, the workers have voted increasingly for the Labour Party. By-elections and municipal elections all demonstrate the flow of political opinion and that flow is behind the Labour Party. The tide is setting in towards a Parliamentary majority for the Labour Party.

Parallel with this political development has proceeded the class collaboration of the Trade Unions with the Government. The defeat of the General Strike and the Miners' Lock-out with the subsequent fettering of the unions by the 1927 Trade Union Act constitute definite political reason for this course of development. But important economic factors have also played their part, not the least of which is the fall in prices tending to enhance the value of real wages and a period of trade improvement.

These latter facts have appeared to lend strength to a theory that the crisis through which we have been living for years is merely a passing crisis within capitalism as distinct from the crisis of capitalism. Indeed the argument goes further. We are informed that the leopard does after all change its spots and capitalism has changed its character. " In the past," says Mr. Milne-Bailey, " the predominant feature of economic life has been the scarcity of goods necessary to the well-being or even the existence of mankind " (*Trade Unions and the State*, p. 323). " In fact," he continues, " the whole economic mechanism has been dominated by the fact of the scarcity of economic goods, and only individuals or groups specially favoured by their institutional privilege or by a particular type of ability could transcend this evil. . . . The State was not ' a public service State ' with positive functions " (p. 324).

This " passing of scarcity " theory is the sequel to the extraordinary development in recent years of the technical means of production. This development, we are told, demonstrates *now* that there is no need for poverty to exist in the world. But this is not a twentieth century discovery. To suggest that the great mass of the population of this country or any country where capitalism reigns have been poverty-stricken because of " scarcity " of a natural character will not bear two minutes' examination. There have been famines which have swept great masses of population to their doom through some natural calamity but the great mass of poverty in the world is simply due to the robbery of the masses who have produced the goods, by those who have owned the goods and the means whereby they were produced. That may seem a crude mode of exposition of the economic facts, but it is nevertheless true.

The general level of life prior to the industrial revolution in this country, for example, may not have been high compared with the twentieth century, but the devastation in the condition of the masses wrought by the Industrial Revolution stands on record. A technological revolution

took place at that time which called forth pæans
of praise from the Macaulays, but " scarcity "
spread itself at the base of the social pyramid
whilst riches filled up the pockets of the private
owners of the means of production at its apex.
It is incontestable that had the technical
revolution been carried forward on the basis of
a socialist revolution, then there would " have
been no scarcity ". The proof of this is out-
standingly clear in this century in the Russian
revolution. The industrial revolution in Russia
has been carried through by Socialism and has
swept unemployment before it, as with a mighty
broom, while laying secure the foundation for
comfort for all.

If further proof were needed then it is to be
found in the fact that the greater the technological revolution of to-day, the greater become
the social contrasts—the polarity of riches and
poverty—the greater the army of unemployed.
The economic mechanism has not been and is
not animated by any " scarcity " theory. It has
been, and is, dominated by private property
relations which, the more science is applied to the
technical side of production, increase the social
contrasts—the poverty and the riches.

We have now reached that remarkable position

in this country when " *Ten per cent* of the
population, getting over £250 a year, obtain
nearly *half* the national income ; *fifteen per
cent*, getting between £250–£159 a year, receive
almost exactly equivalent in proportion to its
numbers ; *while the great bulk of the people,
seventy-five per cent* of the population, with
incomes ranging from £159–nil a year, receives
less than two-fifths of the whole " (L. Ben-
jamin, *The Position of the Middle-Class Worker
in the Transition to Socialism*, p. 6).

The theory that we are just entering an
epoch of abundance in which wealth can
stream downwards to all the poverty-stricken
homes of the world, to wash out its misery
with abundance, without breaking with the
claims of private property, is untenable.

Nor can the immediate " improvement " of
trade be regarded as the beginning of a new
phase of the organic development of the
forces of production. This is not the place
to give an exhaustive economic analysis, but
I venture to assert that the upward trend of
the curve of trade is the most " artificial " and
calamitous in its significance of any since the
war of 1914–18. It is the direct sequel to
the development of " economic nationalism "

expressing itself in tariffs, quotas, currency manipulation, etc., leading to the saturation of the home markets by "home producers" and more intense rivalry in international economic relations.

The saturation of the home market must of necessity stimulate and intensify international competition. This in turn must stimulate war preparations. The certainty of a new stage of the economic crisis arising from the same fundamental causes which produced the previous crisis is, therefore, clear for all to see if they but care to look. If war is held off, then a steep plunge in the world of commercial production stands not far ahead : if war intervenes, then we are face to face with the calamity of calamities.

The future of the Trade Unions in relation to the State consequently assumes a problematical character. Should the new stage of the economic crisis break the "boomlet" before the general election comes, there is no doubt whatever that a further impetus would be given to the political side of the Trade Unions and the possibility of the return of a Labour majority to the House of Commons would become almost a certainty. Such a possibility is not ruled out even if the election takes place before the break in the trade " boom " arrives.

Should there not be a Labour Government as the result of the next elections, there is little doubt that the government ensuing would be a short-lived government. From the day of its taking office its majority would be in jeopardy. The demands of the Labour Movement would increase. The pressure from outside would increase. The consciousness of ascendancy in the ranks of the working class would inevitably sharpen the pace towards change, and therefore sharpen the relations between the Labour Movement and the opposing parties. *Unless some unconstitutional or extra-Parliamentary methods are adopted by the forces standing for the old order*, or some new unexpected split takes place in the ranks of the Labour Movement, or war intervenes, it is safe to say that the historical stage is set for the coming of a Labour Government committed in broad declaration to Socialism.

Then will arrive the critical hour in the history of the Labour Movement. Will it advance to Socialism or temporize once more with some form of " Rooseveltian New Deal " as expressed in the Trade Union Congress resolution I have already quoted ? If the latter, then an internal crisis in the whole movement will be inevitable and its fate will depend upon its ability to change its leaders from within in order to tackle the problems demanding a socialist solution. Failing that, the degeneration which befell the German Labour Movement will follow, with an equally disastrous sequel. A Party and a Movement which fails to advance decisively to the tasks which its whole preceding history has been preparing at the moment when life offers it the opportunity to act must crash. This was the fate of labour in Italy and in Germany.

It is not my purpose here to project what would be likely to happen after such a calamity. though I believe that to fail in this way means that all the objective conditions for the rapid advance to Fascism will then have been created. Having sounded the warning note of what is latent in the development of the struggle between the social forces now contending over the body of a decaying system and stressed how disaster can be avoided, it is necessary to show what role the Trade Unions can perform on the basis of the victory of the forces of social progress.

The policy of a socialist government in relation to foreign affairs, the House of Lords, etc., do not come within the scope of this book, although they have an important bearing upon the solving of the problems with which the Trade Unions will be directly concerned. Indeed, all questions which have a bearing upon the problem of attaining power and keeping it have a relationship to the question of the future of the unions. For example, if the defeated parties, representative of the vested interests which Socialism must attack, refuse to accept the will of the people as expressed in a Parliamentary majority and proceed to extra-Parliamentary forms of struggle as in the time of the Irish Home Rule struggle, then the Trade Unions may be called upon to play the role of allies of the Government, facing what is virtually civil war. The Parliamentary conquest of power by Socialism would then either be sealed by a victory over reaction complete and final, or itself be conquered by counter-revolutionary Fascism.

With this aspect of the situation also I do not propose to deal here, although it raises issues and problems which ought to be studied seriously. Here we will deal only with the problems of the unions on the basis of labour having achieved power constitutionally, and having been accepted as the Government which has to introduce Socialism.

From the standpoint of political relationships the Trade Unions and the Government should now be allies in the carrying through of a social revolution. Whilst the Government is not the State it has in its power to use the State providing the majority of the great staff of permanent officials of the Army, Navy, Air Force, Police, Law Courts, Civil Service, etc., in charge of the State machine accept the Government decisions and carry out its orders.

The land, the banks, the mills and mines, the whole machinery of industry are in the hands of private owners, whether dressed up in the garb of company directors, heads of combines, or any other attire. How will these become socialized and how will they be managed ?

If the Government proceeds to take one industry at a time, or presuming that it begins its work by nationalizing the banks and spreads its socialization measures over a period of years, then it must be obvious that for this period, whatever it may be, the Trade Unions can only play the role of general political support to the Government and its traditional role of defender of wages, hours of labour, protector against accidents, purveyor of social insurance in those industries which are not socialized. This would be a dangerous period, especially if the Government, anxious for social peace, becomes as it did in 1929, the means of attacking the Trade Unions. The employers on the one hand pressed by difficulties of competition in a growing crisis of capitalist economy would demand wage reductions and other concessions, the Government, not prepared to socialize the industry immediately, would have to come down on the side of the employers. The complications of delay are surrounded with pitfalls that can be disastrous to Socialism.

An alternative has been proposed for the separation of economics from politics by the creation of a " House of Industry " composed of representatives of the Government, the capitalists, and the Trade Unions. Such an institution, which of necessity would have to control the economic life of the country, would be no solution of the questions before the country. It would, in fact, strip the Government of its power, or merely transfer its problems from the House of Commons to an outside body and make the problems more difficult of solution by the invasion of the representatives of contradictory interests.

There is a further alternative proposal, namely that of reconstructing the machinery of controlled capitalism of the War period as transitory machinery towards socialization. It is argued that what was done by the capitalists during the War in the interests of the capitalists can be done by a Labour Government in the interests of Socialism. There is a certain plausibility in this argument. It is certainly the logical application of the resolution of the Brighton Trades Union Congress. It avoids the direct attack on private property and appears to give many gains to the workers. But experience has already shown that a rising standard of life and the retention of private property are incompatible.

A prospective Labour Government appears, therefore, to have no means of avoiding or delaying the approach to the revolutionary issues their election implies. There is no lengthy breathing space between the time of getting power and having to face the problems of socialization. A Labour Government has to be socialist and face its tasks quickly and decisively. If not, then it produces an internal

M

crisis in the Labour Movement which settles the issue in favour of decisive socialist action, or it perishes at the hands of anti-socialists, who will throughout this period have been anything but passive observers.

Assuming, therefore, that the Labour Government becomes a socialist government proceeding promptly with the socialization of the banks, land, and industry, a number of outstanding questions remain to be answered. Will the Trade Unions become organs of the State ? If not, what will be their relationship to it ?

These questions were once discussed in Soviet Russia in the early days of the Russian Revolution. Trotsky put forward the proposal that the Trade Unions must become organs of the State. Lenin opposed the proposal and Lenin's ideas carried the day. He argued that the Trade Unions must remain free, voluntary organizations defending the workers' conditions and interests in a free alliance with the workers' government. This was also a time of transition to Socialism when a considerable part of soviet economy was still capitalist, operating under the supervision of a workers' State.

The essential difference between the two views has an important bearing on the future

of society in all countries. Trotsky was obsessed with the idea of State power as a per-
manency and therefore sought to incorporate
all the workers' mass organizations within
the State machine. Lenin, on the other hand,
kept clearly before him the vision of a society
of freely co-operating functional institutions
and the " withering away of the State ". The
Soviet State was regarded by him as a class
weapon for the suppression of the capitalist
elements of society. With the abolition of classes
the necessity for a State power vanishes, for
who is there then to be held down or
suppressed? In Lenin's view a socialist State has
a double function to perform. It has, on the one
hand, to overcome the opposition to Socialism
and, at the same time, to develop the organs for
the " administration of things ". The failure
to appreciate these two functions of a socialist
State had led to much confusion both in regard
to the history and position of the Trade Unions
in the Soviet Union and to the future of the
State.

Mr. Milne-Bailey is a big offender in this
matter. Like many others he does not recognize
what is really the most remarkable transformation in the development of institutions

yet witnessed in the history of mankind—a
transformation which throws a flood of light
upon the probable course of events in other
countries. " Superficially," says Mr. Bailey,
" it might seem that Soviet Russia has
solved the problem of Trade Unions' conflicts with the State by establishing a powerful
dictatorship which gives the unions a place,
albeit a subordinate one, in the mechanism
of government, and keeps them there, partly
by propaganda and partly by sheer force."
The only evidence he offers to justify this
summary of the situation is a series of quotations
from resolutions defining the position of workshop committees and Trade Unions in relation
to the control of industry at different stages in
the history of the revolution. But not one tittle
of evidence does he provide of the unions being
held " by sheer force ". Why the same people
who control the State should repress and use
sheer force against themselves in the Trade
Unions passes comprehension. One may not
like the " dictatorship of the proletariat " but
at least it is necessary to recognize that it is
not directed against itself but against a class
or classes that have been deprived of " their
dictatorship ".

As for the evolution of the Soviet State and the Trade Unions, is that not to be expected ? The real question is : What is the character of the changes since the beginning of the revolution until the present period and in what direction are they tending ?

It must be recognized that the first problem of any revolution is the conquest of political power ; the second, the consolidation and defence of that power ; the third, to set the forces of production working on the principles of the new regime, however improvised and temporary the means ; the fourth, the development of the institutions created by the revolution in accordance with the aims of the revolution. Many other things could be said about the requirements of the new order, but these will suffice to illustrate the changes under review.

The soviets or workers' councils were in the first stage of the revolution little more than enlarged strike committees representative of the great masses of workers, peasants, and soldiers. When all political power passed into their hands they had not only to develop a new state apparatus, and defend the revolution against counter-revolution, they had also to make sure of their conquest of the factories, mills and mines, and the landed estates.

What other means were to hand other than workshop committees to " clear out the old gang " or assume responsibility where they had fled ? This was a matter of necessity. But did any responsible body think that this was therefore the last word in the organization of " workers' control of industry " ? Whoever thought so and whoever takes such an improvisation as the criterion of " workers' control of industry " is simply a child in the school of politics.

But Mr. Bailey follows with a series of quotations which show, not as he endeavours to make out, that the workers have lost the control of industry, but that they have applied the functional principle to the development of their institutions. They have created trusts which are held responsible for one aspect of the control of industry, for example a metal trust, steel trust, textile trust, etc., which are held responsible for the management of the industries. But they are *workers'* trusts, organs for particular phases of management and direction, the ordering of raw materials, the direction of the process of manufacture, the disposal of the products through other institutions. The trusts have replaced the capitalists in so far as the directive and managerial aspect of their functions are concerned, but they have not continued their exploiting function. This has been abolished. A workers' trust, therefore, is not something over and above the workers but a workers' institution for the administration of industry, an application of the functional principle in " the administration of things ".

Mr. Bailey quotes the following : " In the U.S.S.R. a sharp distinction is made between the function of managing industry, and the function of organizing and defending the interests of the workers and employees in industry. The former function is in the hands of the national economic authorities of the trust and industry management, and the latter function is in the hands of the workers' organizations and the Trade Unions."

" Later," he says, " the unions were made to take a still more subordinate part in the industrial mechanism. An order of the Central Committee of the Communist Party in 1929 laid it down that ' the Trade Union organization while defending the economic and cultural interests of the workers, must collaborate

energetically in increasing their output—they
must not in any way interfere in the management or place obstacles in the way '. Workers
were," he adds, " by order of the Labour Commissariat, 21st May, 1931, forbidden to take part
during working hours in the activities of
soviets, Trade Unions, co-operatives, etc.,
or in any other duties not directly concerned
with production.   Thus, the unions were
deprived of their positions of equality with all
other organs of the State and became a sub-
sidiary part of the state machinery " (*Trade
Unions and the State*, p. 301).

It is difficult to understand what is meant
by " equality with all other organs of the State ".
Is it meant that there is no equality if there is
differentiation of function. The trusts belong
to the workers, the Trade Unions belong to
the workers, the State belongs to the workers.
The State is the central political authority
initiating, developing new organs of administration, regulating those already developed,
transforming society into a classless working
community, and the custodians of the defence
against the dangers from the world of capitalism.
The organs of industrial, social and cultural
administration now developing as co-ordinated

self-governing institutions, are the permanent institutions for the " administration of things ". The State is the transitory temporary authority aiding the working community to advance along the lines of functional democracy, vanishing as the class enemies internally and externally disappear.

Naturally, just so long as the socialist government, even after it has established a classless society within its frontiers, has to face a hostile world of capitalism, all institutions, no matter with what aspect of economic and social life they deal, must be subordinate to the requirements of the State. Nothing is clearer than this fact in the history of the Soviet Union. Had the Soviet not had to face a fierce class war internally, a war of intervention by capitalist states, and a perpetual threat of further wars after the first interventions had been defeated, the rate of the rise of the standard of life of the peoples of the Soviet would have been far greater.

The external world in this respect has governed the internal life of the Soviet and the rule and power of the State. The war danger has governed both the rate and nature of the industrial transformation of the Soviet Union enormously. It is only necessary to remark

that the £700,000,000 defence Budget of the
current year could have been diverted to social
development were it not for the threatening
war from outside. This it is which gives the
State in the transition period to world Socialism
its preponderant importance and obscures the
evolution of the means for " the administration
of things " which proceeds under the guardian-
ship of the socialist State.

It is this evolution of the permanent means
of administration of the classless society which
distinguishes the position and function of the
socialist State and consequently the relations
of the Trade Unions thereto, from the State of
Fascism.   In the latter, all institutions are
organs of the capitalist State. The authoritative
state is everything ;   permanently dominating
all activities.

The corporations are co-operations of conflicting interests held in the grip of the State,
permanent, supreme, the arbiter over all
contradictions, the god of capitalist authority
over a helot class of toilers.

A Labour Government in this country, intent
on achieving Socialism, will, therefore, have
before it the same fundamental problem that
faced the Soviet Government, though in far

more favourable conditions. Its tasks will consist of developing the institutions and organs of administration which belong permanently to the new order, and creating new institutions of administration. Its guiding principle will be that of functional administration on the basis of social ownership. On this basis and with the above principle in operation the Trade Unions will not be organs of the State but its allies.

The State will not be regarded as the permanent institution, but as the transitional authority destined to pass away with the coming of world Socialism. Its internal responsibility will be that of transforming Britain into a classless society.

In this society the Trade Unions have definite functions, not as fighting institutions against exploitation, but as administrative organs in the democratic self-government of industry. What this means in greater detail we will now consider.

CHAPTER IX

THE FUTURE OF THE TRADE UNIONS IN INDUSTRY

HAVING stated the principles of the new relationship between the Trade Unions and the State which arise immediately the character of the State is changed from that of the weapon for the defence of private property to the weapon of social property, the way is clear for an examination of the new scope and powers of the Trade Unions as allies of the socialist State.

Up to this time the Trade Unions have been (*a*) the defenders of wage rates, hours of labour, factory conditions, etc., a brake on the rate of exploitation of the workers ; (*b*) the custodians of certain forms of social insurance, such as unemployment pay, sick pay, old age pensions, or superannuation ; (*c*) " consultants " with regard to the general development and organization of the economic life of the country. This latter feature of their activity has taken

the form of collaboration with the employers
and the Government, by means such as the
Mond–Turner discussions, joint policy for-
mulating with the employers' federations,
attendance at economic conferences convened
by the Government and the League of
Nations.

Naturally the coming of a socialist government would call for the adoption of new
methods of running industry. But whether the
socialist government be parliamentary or soviet
it could not itself undertake the administration
of industry. The Government is the political
authority for effecting the change from private
ownership to social ownership. It is the centre
of political power for settling the question of
ownership in the name of the new society.
Having settled the ownership question it has
to create the means for the administration of
industry.

How the question of ownership is settled will
determine the means whereby the new method
of administration of industry will be created.
If the transition is through the securing of a
parliamentary socialist government accepted
by the minority defeated in the elections, then
the first step would be the creation of a National

Economic Council for the co-ordination and direction of industry.

If, however, the change from one system to another meets with the stubborn resistance of vested interests and the issue has to be settled by civil conflict, then the new mechanism will arise in a different way. The direct mass conquest of ownership will have to precede the development of forms of administration and the factory committees will be called upon to play the same role as in the Russian Revolution. "Workers' control of industry" would then be a political slogan of the workers in the direct fight for possession. That, of course, is a class political fight and not necessarily parliamentary in form.

Both Mr. Milne-Bailey in his book *Trade Unionism and the State*, and Mr. Herbert Morrison in his book the *Socialization of Transport*, misinterpret the evolution of the forms of "workers' control" in the Soviet Union and assume that workers' control is steadily abandoned because the Trade Unions and the State created "trusts", assume different functions the farther away we get from the first months of the revolution. The fact is there has been no abandonment of workers' control.

Ownership and control are inseparable and the workers of Russia have not surrendered ownership, they have changed the forms of administration of industry and government on the principles of functional democracy inherent within all socialist theory. That this evolution of administration of socialized industry has deviated from preconceived notions of how it should be done was only to be expected. The deviations, however, are not so remarkable as the amount of revolutionary socialist theory which proved correct in practice, every step of which was without precedent.

If, however, my analysis of the possibility of a parliamentary socialist government be correct, the starting point for the "workers' control of industry" will be different from that of Soviet Russia, the evolution of its forms of development will be different, though the goal may be the same.

Neither a soviet government, nor a parliamentary socialist government can administer industry without creating special institutions for the purpose. The socialist government has to start from scratch. Having achieved political power through the parliamentary franchise, the problem of administering industry will be

presented to the socialist government and the
workers in industry in an entirely different way
from that in the history of the Russian Revolution, always providing that the capitalists accept
the parliamentary decision without creating a
pro-slavery rebellion and civil war.

Once more, therefore, assuming the acceptance of the rapid transition to Socialism, the
first step of the socialist government must be
to create a National Economic Council, representative of the socialized banks and industries,
trade unions and co-operatives, selected experts
in economics, etc. This will be the first step
towards the social administration of things.

That such a council cannot work as an *ad hoc*
body is obvious. It will have to form its
planning commissions, sub-committees, and
departments, and be built up generally on the
principle of a federation of industries in accordance with the structure of the industries which
the council is called upon to administer. No
industry can be run as an isolated unit but
only as a co-ordinated part of the rest of industry.
Hence the necessity for the federal principle
to be applied and the general co-ordination to
be effected in a National Economic Council.

This council will be responsible for the planning of industry and its administration. Its plans, of course, must receive the approval of the Government and Parliament which represent the political authority for the transition to the new society. Leading members of the Government must be in charge of the National Economic Council and be held responsible to the cabinet.

In the first stages the work of the National Economic Council will fall into two main divisions. On the one hand, its task will be the planned reorganization of the socialized industries and, on the other hand, the control of non-socialized industries. Although the problems attached to the first task are different from those of the second, they are closely related. It must be obvious that any attempt to plan the development of the economic life of the country without the National Economic Council having all the economic forces under its control, including the import and export of goods, must be doomed to failure. Planned economy and economic anarchy cannot live side by side in a single community. Anarchy in production must inevitably shatter all plans as every attempt to develop "planned capitalism" in the jungle of the competitive relations of capitalism has already proved. However much, therefore, of industry is immediately socialized, control of the non-socialized industry must be an essential part of the planned transition to Socialism.

The National Economic Council will, accordingly, have its departments for the control of foreign trade, its investment boards, and its planning commissions as part of its machinery for the administration of industry. It will control imports and exports, regulate the flow of investments both in the socialized and non-socialized industries, and then bring order into the development of the economic life of the community in place of the stupidities of the tariff system and the gambling of the Stock Exchange.

Just as it will be necessary to co-ordinate the industries nationally so there will be the need for effective co-operation with the various regions of the country each of which will have its economic council constructed on similar lines. They will be appointed by the National Economic Council and responsible to it for the carrying through of the general plan.

It will be asked from whence are these

bodies chosen and who can remove them if unsatisfactory, etc. The answer is that the personnel will be nominated by the Trade Unions, local authorities, co-operatives, the Labour Party, and the Government, on the basis of their special knowledge, administrative ability and loyalty to the fulfilment of the socialist plan. They will be removed when proven unsatisfactory by the National Economic Council, or the committees of the council responsible for the appointment, on representation from any of the organizations which have the power of nomination. The selective principle applied in appointment is thus controlled by the elective principle. Thus will industrial democracy begin to work.

It may be argued that the National Economic Council and its industrial sections and departments ought really to be the General Council of the Trades Union Congress and the executives of the Trade Unions after they have been transformed into industrial unions. Whatever the future may have in store it must be obvious that, if political power comes to Labour in the way described, the existing structure and functions of the Trade Unions are not cut out for such an undertaking. There are hundreds

of Trade Unions. The total membership
is not more than four and a half millions, as
compared with a working population of more
than sixteen millions. The officials of the unions
have been elected for totally different purposes.
The great mass of the Trade Union branches
have little relation to the workshops, except
that their members work in them.

Indeed, one of the most urgent tasks of the
Trade Unions is, and will be more so, on the
morrow of the coming of a socialist government,
their transformation into industrial unions to
be inclusive of all who work in industry. At
present they constitute a tremendous reservoir
of energy and skill which can and will be applied
in the workers' administration of industry but
to-day they are not organized with that purpose
in view. Hence the need for change in methods
of organization and the need for a new vision
of their tasks. At the same time, because they
are composed of the workers in industry and with
all their defects represent the great mass who
have the task before them of rebuilding society,
they must be drawn into the National Economic
Council.

The proposal for the handing over of the
administration of industry to the Trade Unions

re-organized as industrial unions is derived, of course, from the theories of the revolutionary industrial unionists.   Once more the whole question turns on the issue of how power passes into the hands of socialists.   Their view was that of the conquest of industry, factory by factory, mill by mill, mine by mine, etc.   Every factory was to them a fortress to be captured for revolutionary industrial unionism until the superstructure of the State could be overthrown by the universal dismissal of the capitalists. It was the route via the workshop and factory committees which either transformed the unions in the process or superseded them by new industrial unions.

Whatever of value there is in the struggle for the transformation of the unions and the vision of an industrial democracy, there is no evidence of the possibility of the workers achieving power in that way. Hence the necessity of facing the fact that the Trade Unions will have to tackle the problems of their transformation largely after the achievement of political power.   It is, therefore, necessary to reject the proposal for the Trades Union Congress and the union executives immediately becoming the National Economic Council, whilst calling

on them and the co-operatives and Labour
organizations to give the maximum of representation within it commensurable with the
necessity to give the experts in all departments
ample scope along with the requirements of
political expediency in carrying through the
policy of the Government.

The central machinery of industrial and
economic planning and administration must
have its corresponding departments in the form
of regional and district councils appointed by
the National Economic Council. Its units of
administration will be the directors and
managerial workers of each enterprise. From
top to bottom the functions of these institutions,
however they be detailed out in the forms of
socialist trusts, etc., will be those of planning,
directing, and managing the economic and
industrial life of the country. They will be
responsible to the Government, the political
authority responsible for the use and transformation of the State in the name of the new
society.

These are the institutions, therefore, which
will arrive at agreements with the Trade
Unions concerning wages and hours of labour
and conditions of employment. The unions

will not drop this function but carry it forward into the new order. The conditions of the new arrangements, however, will be totally different from the present. Instead of being face to face with opponents whose aim is to extract as much profit as possible from the workers, the meeting of the respective organizations will be animated by the same purpose, in that they meet on the common platform of community ownership. Their function will be essentially a scientific, regulative one. It is no longer a war of contending forces each seeking to extract the maximum from the other, but the meeting of departments of the same concern. Whether it will be found easier to work these problems out on a national or local basis remains to be seen. In either case, the principles upon which they work and the mechanism for carrying out this function is the same. The unions will cease to be the instruments for strikes when the property relations which make such activity necessary will have vanished. There is no need for the workers to strike against themselves.

But in the transition period there will be industries that are socialized and industries that remain on a capitalist basis. We may, therefore, expect to witness the Trade Unions performing

two functions—constructing Socialism on the
one hand, and defending workers against the
capitalists on the other. Even so, the position
of the unions can hardly be comparable with
that of the present. Those unions in the
remaining capitalist industry would have the
support of their socialist government. Hence
the strike weapon would be little in evidence
even in the transition where all the forces of
the State are directed towards Socialism.

In the industries not socialized by the
Government, the full moral and political
pressures of the Government must support the
formation of works committees and councils.
By these means the Trade Unions will be able
to exercise a measure of control over conditions
of work to ensure the fulfilment of agreements
between the unions and the employers, and
prepare for the socialization and full control
of the industry.

The other functions of social insurance, for
old age, sickness, unemployment (so long as
there is any) insurance, the organization of social
welfare, can be taken over completely from the
State apparatus. This has already happened in
the Soviet Union. In 1933, the whole budget
of £155,000,000 previously administered by

the Commissariat of Labour (a similar government department to that of the Ministry of
Labour in this country) was transferred in its
entirety to the Trade Unions. The Trade
Unions of this country have had a rich experience
in this kind of administration and have developed
an administrative staff for the purpose which it
would be difficult to improve upon. Whether
the Trade Unions could take over this work
completely until transformed into industrial
unions is doubtful. But once it was indicated
that this was to be done it would give a powerful
impetus to the process of transformation of the
unions along the lines required.

This is not all that is required for the
transformation. Workshop organization must
accompany the developments I have outlined,
indeed must be the basis upon which the transformation is effected. Unless this is done the
actual operation of the agreements and control
of the processes of production will not be
possible.

It will be necessary for the workers in each
factory to elect their works' council. In small
factories this may be done at a mass meeting
of all the workers : in larger factories by
means of departmental meetings electing their

representatives. With the transformation of
the unions into industrial unions these will be
the units of the unions corresponding to the
branch meetings of to-day. Although, at first,
not all the workers will be members of the
unions, social pressure, and common interest
and the absence of an alternative basis upon
which to foster non-unionism, will quickly
ensure the vast majority of the workers becoming
members of the unions. It is only necessary
to recall the swift growth of the Trade Unions
in the War period with the absence of unemployment to recognize how much more swiftly the
recruitment would be under the impact of
revolutionary changes and the moral influence
of a socialist government. It will become a
mark of dishonour and counter-revolutionary
sympathies to be a non-unionist in those days.

Here once more in the election of workers'
councils in the factories is the application of
the popular elective principle which in its
operation checks the application of the selective
principle in the appointments to special positions
of responsibility.

What will the workers' council do ? It will
arrange with the management such questions
as the manning of the departments, the transfer

of labour, employment of labour, settle grievances of individual workers ; it will check up the management on the supply of materials and the relations of the management to the rest of the workers, discuss the plans of production prepared by the managerial side of the establishment and the fulfilment of the plans. It must be remembered constantly that the workers' council and the management will be no longer representatives of opposing forces but will be functionaries of a common interest and purpose. The works council will not therefore be simply a grievance bureau but a part of the mechanism of workers' control of industry, as keenly interested in the work of the management as the management itself. The Council will not be an " interfering " body but a popular democratic means of ensuring the harmonious working of all engaged in the productive process. It will make nominations for various posts requiring technical skill but the directorate will decide. Managers will be managers and directors will be directors who will be held responsible for the decisions they make and are expected to make as functionaries of the common will.

Such is the general structure of the machinery

of administration which appears to me to be the natural evolution to socialist forms of administration arising from the determined effort of a socialist government elected through Parliament. It would not supersede Parliament popularly elected, but be responsible to it provided the struggle for political power to effect the economic change in society had not forced upon society a new political form. But, as I have repeatedly emphasized, the whole economic apparatus must be subordinate to the political authority of society until the classes have merged into the classless society within our frontiers and beyond them.

It is now possible to see how the great change will affect the position of the rank and file workers, of technicians, and professions. The economic aspect is not the province of this book.

Sufficient to say that the socialization of the means of production alone provides the means whereby to close " the scissors " of production and consumption, i.e. to effect the transformation in the distribution of wealth so that they correspond to each other. It is by this means and this alone that economic security, regularity of income, and hours of labour, provision for inadvertent events for all, can be met.

The importance of this economic revolution in the life of society cannot be measured. Great though it may be, no less great will be the change effected in the spiritual stature of man. All that is meant by this change can only be fully realized by him who has been a slave and is now free.

Dr. H. F. Ward, in his most interesting and valuable book *In Place of Profit*, recalls the following incident which occurred in a Soviet factory.

> " We had a row here last week. The director changed the machines around without consulting the workers. You should have seen what they did to him. They called a meeting and put him on the carpet. They said, ' Who do you think you are, changing these machines around without consulting us ? This is *our* factory, not yours.' "

In this briefly recorded incident is the essence of everything that is meant by social ownership and the worker's control. These things are not mine nor thine but OURS. " No master, high or low." Co-operation in a common purpose. Division of work and functional responsibility co-ordinated and applied to the conquest of the machines, the tools, materials, and all that enters into the productive process.

To those who have been accustomed to command and be obeyed such a prospect as this is appalling. To those who work at the bench, on the machine, in the mill and mine, and have felt the overwhelming pressure of economic power behind the words of command, it is the vision of what emancipation means. Let us see how it works still more closely.

Take, for example, an engineering factory. Under the existing regime it has its boards of directors, managers, experts, draftsmen, accountants, costing departments, speedmen, detectives, chargehands, skilled, semi-skilled, and unskilled workers, men and women. All are subordinate to the driving motive of profit. Quality of production, human dignity, joy in work are sacrificed to profit. Fear of dismissal, brutal driving, nerve-racking anxiety, suspicions, murmurings, sneaking, spying, competition for jobs and favoured places, characterize human association. The machine towers over men, women, and youth, as a fierce slave driver burning up their energy at an ever-faster rate and throwing them on the industrial scrap

heap irrespective of their fate.   The ethics of
the jungle and the tyranny of the machine in
the production of profit are supreme in the
world of capitalist economy.

The same engineering factory in the world of
socialism, run on the principles outlined, would
also have its directors, its managers, its experts,
accountants, draftsmen, costing clerks.   But the
speed merchants would be absent.   The
detectives would be absent.   The fears of
dismissal would be absent.   The profit motive
would be absent.

The managers and directors would be
appointed by the National Economic Council or
its representatives. These would be responsible
for the employment of the experts, the draftsmen, the accountants, etc., and the general
staffing of the factory in consultation with the
works council.   The works council would be
elected by the workers in the factory.   The
council would not be full time officials as
a rule, though according to the size of the
factory it may be necessary to have some of
their number engaged in this way. The council
as a whole would be composed of workers
" on the job ", at the bench, on the machine.
This is the industrial union at work.

It would ensure and control the application of the National and local agreements between the unions and the National Economic Council. The council would hold joint meetings with the management to discuss the plan of work for developing the initiative of the workers in every department of administration to ensure both qualitative and quantitative standards of production. Developing the consciousness of their common ownership of industry and what is produced by it, their approval, their approach to all questions become fundamentally different. Directors and managers cease to be menacing figures who hold the power of dismissal over the heads of the rest of the workers. They become fellow workers who are held responsible for a high function by the workers in the factories and the rest of the community.

Directors and managers will have to be leaders of ability and not merely technical experts with the capacity of the bully. They will be held responsible for the supply of materials for the processes of production undertaken by the particular concern in which they are in charge, for efficiency in administration, and expressing the spirit of co-operation in a common purpose.

The directors will receive the general plan of work from the National Economic Council. This plan will be worked over by the managerial staff and departmentalized so that every section of the factory can understand what the collective social will expects as their contribution to the common purpose. This plan will be submitted to the workers through the workers' councils in the factory so that each worker can examine the plan and check the details of the work to be undertaken. Through meetings and discussions the men on the job will check the plan, revise the plan, and control the plan when agreed upon.

This process is well described by F. Ward. He writes describing the method of work in the Soviet Union :—

" As the plan comes down through the factory it gets broken into smaller units and set for shorter times. The planning department will work it out for a three months' period, the planning brigade in a shop for a month, and the working brigade for ten or five days and sometimes each day. Also the figures that go back to headquarters become much more exact as the workers fill them in from their experience. For instance,

o

a young engineer in an electrical factory
tells me the plan will call for ten million
lamps at 42 kopecks, the workers plan may
total up to nearly fifteen million lamps at 30
kopecks. Why ? Because the drafter, not
knowing the machine, puts down 1,000 parts
for it, the worker says, ' We—the machine
and I—can do 1,223,' because he knows just
what he has been averaging."

That's true enough. No one can estimate
what can be done better than the man on the
job when he is harnessed to the joy of achievement, free from the nagging fears of competitive
capitalism. No one can measure the joy in
turning out a good job free from the interruptions
of a " speed merchant " whose sole desire is
output.

Much nonsense is written to-day about the
" tyranny of the machine ". It is not the
machine that is the tyrant but the " profit-
motived system " in which it has to be worked
that is the tyrant. There is no greater joy than
the manipulation of a fine piece of machinery
providing the man who has to work it is a free
man, and therefore master of the machine.
Nothing is more destroying to a craftsman using
the tools of production than the capitalist

foreman's interruption, " Here, that job isn't for exhibition ! Don't put so damned much finish on it."

Even the " belt system " of production can become a pleasure when handled by a team of workers collectively interested in it and its products because it is theirs.

Thus the " workers' control of industry " I visualize is not that of a mere formal representation of the Trade Union officials upon some board of directors, it is the active continual control of the workers on the job in the fullest meaning of the word. This is functional democracy at work on the basis of the social ownership of the means of production—the only basis upon which such a democracy is realizable. It was by these means that the Five Year Plan of the Soviet Union was carried through in four years. The plan was revised from below in the manner I have indicated. And this was done with an untrained working class that had to be educated for disciplined factory work as they went along.

What it would mean in a country like ours, with a hundred and fifty years of industrialization behind it and a vast army of workers and technicians whose skill and powers of production are still unmeasured to release this energy and harness it to the new methods and new aims, it is impossible to compute.

But along this path it is clear that the Trade Unions will rapidly change from instruments of struggle against exploitation into administrative organs of a self-governing classless community in which man is free and master of the machine.

INDEX

Printed in Great Britain by Stephen Austin & Sons, Ltd., Hertford.

For Product Safety Concerns and Information please contact our EU
representative GPSR@taylorandfrancis.com
Taylor & Francis Verlag GmbH, Kaufingerstraße 24, 80331 München, Germany